"As Christians, we talk a lot about faith but perhaps too little about doubt. This book reminds us that the Bible talks about both. With the warmth and honesty of a pastor and the wisdom and depth of a theologian, Ryken leads the reader to a renewed and refreshed hope in the truths of God without minimizing the dark challenges of our world. Read it and be encouraged. And then give it to a friend."

Michael J. Kruger, President and Professor of New Testament, Reformed Theological Seminary, Charlotte

"Doubt, a common Christian experience, is sometimes stigmatized in the church. As a result, many believers feel ashamed of their doubts and struggle with them in secret. In this wise and pastoral book, Philip Ryken reminds us how many biblical heroes struggled with doubts. He gives helpful counsel for how we can work through our doubts to arrive at a more rugged and enduring faith. For anyone who struggles with doubt, this book will serve as not only a light to their path but a comfort and balm to their soul."

Gavin Ortlund, President, Truth Unites; author, *Why God Makes Sense in a World That Doesn't*

"One of the great victories of faith in the life of a believer is coming to an understanding that honest doubt represents opportunity, not defeat. Doubt can cause us to seek answers from God and his word that will ultimately strengthen our faith. In this compelling book, Philip Ryken encourages the reader not to run from doubt but instead to grow through it, just as the biblical characters he describes did."

Ed Stetzer, Dean, Talbot School of Theology

"Do you experience suffering, intellectual doubt, moral confusion, or times when it seems God is not there or doesn't care? Philip Ryken writes to believers who have doubts and even consider giving up on faith. As a pastoral scholar and spiritual mentor, Ryken is wise and honest, realistic and encouraging. Above all, he is powerfully biblical as he examines and learns from those in Scripture who faced the same doubts we do and came through them reaffirmed in and reawakened to God's loving presence."

Rick Richardson, Professor and Luis Palau Endowed Chair of Evangelism, Wheaton College; author, *You Found Me*

"Every person will eventually face the abyss of doubt—about God's fairness, about miracles, about God's plans. Philip Ryken's *I Have My Doubts* is the flaming light we need in those dark, lonely times. It's biblical. It's insightful. And it will feed, nourish, and warm your soul."

Sam Chan, head trainer and mentor, EvQ School of Evangelism, City Bible Forum; author, *How to Talk about Jesus (without Being That Guy)*

"Because we Christians don't think we're allowed to have doubts, the moment they arise, we panic. In *I Have My Doubts*, Philip Ryken shares ten stories of biblical characters whose doubts led to flourishing faith. He pastorally reminds us that we are not alone in our doubts, that our doubts do not diminish God, and that all we need to endure is enough faith to take the very next step in following Jesus. We can both believe and find help in our unbelief!"

Juan R. Sanchez, Senior Pastor, High Pointe Baptist Church, Austin, Texas; author, *Seven Dangers Facing Your Church*

"Doubt is everywhere—in politics, media, science, and, of course, the Christian faith. In these ten biblical vignettes about doubt, Ryken provides readers with a path to Christian confidence that refuses to minimize the reality of today's spiritual uncertainties. Ryken does this, ultimately, by reminding us of the one who holds on to us even when we feel unable to hold on to him."

John Dickson, Jean Kvamme Distinguished Professor of Biblical Studies and Public Christianity, Wheaton College; Host, *Undeceptions* podcast

"In *I Have My Doubts*, Philip Ryken thoughtfully reminds us that uncertainty is not antithetical to faith and, moreover, can be fruitfully constitutive of a faithful life. Drawing from a variety of biblical narratives, he reflects on uncertainties that have accompanied Christian pilgrimage throughout the ages. Encouraging readers to 'doubt their doubts,' this book is a refreshing reminder that the flourishing life of a Christ follower materializes not by eschewing all skepticism but by focusing on Christ in the midst of our doubt."

Kevin Brown, President, Asbury University

I Have My Doubts

Other Crossway Books by Philip Ryken

Beauty Is Your Destiny: How the Promise of Splendor Changes Everything

Christian Worldview: A Student's Guide

The Doctrines of Grace: Rediscovering the Evangelical Gospel
(with James Montgomery Boice)

Ecclesiastes: Why Everything Matters

Exodus: Saved for God's Glory

Grace Transforming

Is Jesus the Only Way?

Jeremiah and Lamentations: From Sorrow to Hope

Kingdom, Come!

King Solomon: The Temptations of Money, Sex, and Power

Liberal Arts for the Christian Life

Love of Loves in the Song of Songs

Loving Jesus More

Loving the Way Jesus Loves

Our Triune God: Living in the Love of the Three-in-One
(with Michael LeFebvre)

The Prayer of Our Lord

When Trouble Comes

I Have My Doubts

How God Can Use Your Uncertainty
to Reawaken Your Faith

Philip Ryken

CROSSWAY®

WHEATON, ILLINOIS

Library of Congress Cataloging-in-Publication Data

Names: Ryken, Philip Graham, 1966– author.
Title: I have my doubts : how God can use your uncertainty to reawaken your faith / Philip Ryken.
Description: Wheaton, Illinois : Crossway, 2024. | Includes bibliographical references and index.
Identifiers: LCCN 2023042466 (print) | LCCN 2023042467 (ebook) | ISBN 9781433593390 (trade paperback) | ISBN 9781433593413 (epub) | ISBN 9781433593406 (pdf)
Subjects: LCSH: Trust in God—Christianity. | Trust—Religious aspects. | Belief and doubt—Biblical teaching.
Classification: LCC BV4637 .R77 2024 (print) | LCC BV4637 (ebook) | DDC 231—dc23/eng/20240308
LC record available at https://lccn.loc.gov/2023042466
LC ebook record available at https://lccn.loc.gov/2023042467

Crossway is a publishing ministry of Good News Publishers.

V P					33	32	31	30	29	28	27	26	25	24
15	14	13	12	11	10	9	8	7	6	5	4	3	2	1

To Anna June Ryken,
with the prayer that growing faith
will triumph over troubling doubts
in your walk with Jesus

Contents

Preface   *xi*

1   Doubting God's Trustworthy Word   *1*
     Eve in the Garden of Eden

2   Doubting God's Saving Promise   *17*
     Sarah under the Oak Trees

3   Doubting God's Missional Call   *33*
     Moses at the Burning Bush

4   Doubting God's Supernatural Protection   *47*
     Elisha's Servant at Dothan

5   Doubting God's Abundant Generosity   *63*
     Naomi on the Road to Bethlehem

6   Doubting God's Basic Fairness   *81*
     Asaph outside God's Temple

7   Doubting God's Loving Care   *99*
     Jeremiah in Prison

8   Doubting God's Miraculous Healing   *119*
     The Father in the Crowd

9   Doubting God's Resurrection Power   *137*
    Thomas in the Upper Room

10   Doubting Your Doubts   *153*
    Peter on the Sea of Galilee

    General Index   *167*
    Scripture Index   *173*

Preface

IF WE WERE SITTING TOGETHER RIGHT NOW—just the two of us, you and I—I would lean forward and say: "Can I tell you something? I need to confide in someone."

You might lean forward a little, too, and say: "Sure. Tell me anything."

Then I would share my secret, speaking barely above a whisper: "Sometimes I have my doubts."

There, I said it. And if you raised your eyebrow in the shape of a question mark, I would say it again, only this time I would be more explicit: "What I mean to tell you is that sometimes I have my spiritual doubts."

What would you do next? And what would you say? Maybe you would slump back in your chair and say, "Yeah, me too; I have some doubts of my own."

As a lifelong follower of Jesus Christ, I have many days when my mind and heart are filled with faith. Of course I do! I know that God is there—my Creator. I experience the loving presence of his Holy Spirit. I am convinced that the Bible is the living word of God. I believe that Jesus died for my sins and rose again.

I have full confidence that I am forgiven. My heart's desire is to give God the glory he deserves. I know that the one true and living God is fair and just. His promises are certain and secure. He has a good plan for my life. He will keep me safe. He loves me! One day very soon, God will heal my heartbreak, and I will live forever in his beautiful house. This is what I believe, and I hope you believe it too.

But this does not mean that I never have my doubts—we all do. Sometimes I wonder if God is there; I scarcely feel his presence. I wonder whether certain parts of the Bible are true. I am not completely convinced that someone like me can ever be forgiven. Nor am I totally sure that I can trust God to do what he says. Is he good? *Does* he love me? Will he heal me and protect me? Is there really a heaven after all?

Sometimes the questions come faster than the answers. And then I wonder how to live with my doubts. Can a believer who is sometimes skeptical still walk with God? Is there a God-honoring way to follow the advice that famed journalist Eric Sevareid gave in his memorable final *CBS Evening News* commentary in 1977 and "retain the courage of one's doubts as well as one's convictions"?[1]

To help answer these questions, this short book tells ten stories about doubt that also prove to be stories of credible faith. The men and women who carried these normal, everyday doubts never gave up on God, and he never gave up on them either. Listening to, learning from, and then living out the lessons of their stories can strengthen our faith. Their experiences can serve as a guide to help us work through the wide range of doubts that most of

---

1 "Sevareid Gives His Valedictory," *New York Times*, December 1, 1977, https://www.nytimes.com/.

us experience at some point in our earthly pilgrimage—doubts about God that lead to discouragement and hinder our spiritual progress. The experiences of these biblical doubter-believers can also help us care well for the souls of other skeptics by putting Jude verse 22 into practice: "Have mercy on those who doubt." When we show one another this mercy—and learn to hold our beliefs humbly as well as courageously—our faith rises and joy comes again.

My own faith has been strengthened by writing this book. It was a joy to collaborate during the editorial process with Thomas Boehm, David Downing, Jared Falkanger, Becki Henderson, and Jonathan Rockey, who shared wise insights and made careful corrections. Many partners at Crossway also helped to make this book possible. But I owe the greatest debt to Lisa Maxwell Ryken for her faithful support and to the students of Wheaton College, who remain a constant encouragement as they inspire me to do the very best thinking, writing, and preaching that I can.

Now the serpent was more crafty than any other beast of the field that the L<small>ORD</small> God had made. He said to the woman, "Did God actually say, 'You shall not eat of any tree in the garden'?"

<small>GENESIS 3:1</small>

1

Doubting God's Trustworthy Word

Eve in the Garden of Eden

IS THE BIBLE REALLY TRUE? Is God trustworthy enough for us to take him at his word? Sometimes we have our doubts.

In his novel entitled *In the Beauty of the Lilies*, John Updike describes a Presbyterian minister who falls under the influence of critical, skeptical scholarship and abandons his commitment to Christ. Little by little, the Reverend Clarence Arthur Wilmot questioned the central doctrines of the Christian faith. One day, as he sat "in the rectory of the Fourth Presbyterian Church at the corner of Straight Street and Broadway," Wilmot

felt the last particles of his faith leave him. The sensation was distinct—a visceral surrender, a set of dark sparkling bubbles escaping upward. . . . His thoughts had slipped with quicksilver momentum into the recognition, which he had long withstood, that . . . there is no . . . God, nor should there be.

Clarence's mind was like a many-legged, wingless insect that had long and tediously been struggling to climb up the walls of a slick-walled porcelain basin; and now a sudden impatient wash of water swept it down into the drain. *There is no God.*[1]

Wilmot's spiritual struggle and ultimate surrender resulted directly from his doubts about the word of God. Maybe this is true of all our doubts: if we trace them back far enough, we discover that in one way or another they all begin with our skepticism about the Scriptures.

If the Bible is trustworthy, then we have a solid place to stand. We know who made us: the God who in the beginning created the heavens and the earth, and first breathed life into Adam and Eve. We know that despite the evil we bring into the world, God is working all things for good. We know that through the atoning blood of Jesus Christ there is forgiveness for our sin and shame. We know that we have a purpose: to glorify God and proclaim his gospel to the world. We know that God will guide us and protect us as he leads us to glory. We know all this for the simple reason that the Bible tells us so.

Without the Scriptures of the Old and New Testaments, we would only be hoping and guessing. In a book called *The Certainty of Faith*, Dutch theologian Herman Bavinck wrote:

[1] John Updike, *In the Beauty of the Lilies* (New York: Knopf, 1996), 5–6, emphasis original.

In essence, all truths of the Christian faith come to man from the outside. They are known to him only through revelation, and they become his possession only when he accepts them like a child in faith. . . . Not a knowledge gained through personal investigation, argument and proof, through observation and experiment. But a knowledge gained from a reliable witness.[2]

But what if the Bible is *un*reliable? What if it is a *false* witness? What if Jesus never said some or all of the things attributed to him in Scripture? Where would we stand?

Did God Really Say . . . ?

Essentially, this is the same doubt that Satan sowed in the heart and mind of Eve when he spied her alone in the garden of Eden. With malicious intent, the crafty devil said to the woman, "Did God *actually* say, 'You shall not eat of any tree in the garden?'" (Gen. 3:1).

What Satan said to Eve demands careful scrutiny. Although there is such a thing as an honest doubt, notice that the first theological question anyone asked was a deliberate deception. God did *not* say, "You shall not eat of any tree in the garden." As the devil knew full well, what God said was this: "You *may* surely eat of every tree of the garden, but of the tree of the knowledge of good and evil you shall not eat, for in the day that you eat of it you shall surely die" (Gen. 2:16–17). Satan cleverly turned what was primarily a permission into exclusively a prohibition.

2   Herman Bavinck, *The Certainty of Faith* (St. Catherines, ON: Paideia, 1980), 71.

When we have questions about something in the Bible, it is vitally important for us to make sure that we are reading it carefully and know what it really says!

The first part of Eve's reply shows that she had been listening carefully to her Creator. "We *may* eat of the fruit of the trees in the garden," she said (Gen. 3:2). Yet the rest of her answer went beyond the plain word of God. According to Eve, God said, "You shall not eat of the fruit of the tree that is in the midst of the garden"—so far, so good—"neither shall you touch it, lest you die" (Gen. 3:3). Here Eve went too far. God had only forbidden our first parents from *eating* this particular fruit, not from *touching* it. By saying more than God said, Eve put herself in spiritual danger. If we want to stay safe from theological error, we should be careful neither to add to nor subtract from the word of God, but to hold to the line of Scripture.

When his first attack failed, Satan decided to attempt a less subtle stratagem. This time, instead of a deliberate distortion, he uttered an outright contradiction. "You will not surely die," he said. "For God knows that when you eat of it your eyes will be opened, and you will be like God, knowing good and evil" (Gen. 3:4–5). With these unholy words, the liar called God a liar and made him out to be a miser. By forbidding this fruit, God was not protecting Eve from death, Satan alleged, but preventing her from knowing something she had a right to know.

This accusation assumes there is some place where Eve can stand outside of God's moral authority—a neutral vantage point from which she can critique his character and evaluate his instructions. But if God is God, there is no higher standard. When we claim the right to assess the Almighty on our own terms, we are not simply on shaky ground; we are standing nowhere, in a place that simply does not exist.

Sadly, Eve believed the devil's lie. Doubting the truth of God's trustworthy word and believing instead "that the tree was to be desired to make one wise, she took of its fruit and ate" (Gen. 3:6). Eve regretted this moment for the rest of her life. We all do, living as we do in a fallen world. Unfortunately, we see the same story of undue skepticism repeated far too often. People who know what God says start raising some questions—"honest questions," they may call them. But before long they are in open denial, especially about biblical ethics. Thus, a discussion that starts with "Did God actually say?" and "Do I really have to?" ends with "No, he didn't" and "No, I don't!"

We see a decline of biblical confidence happening today in the United States. According to *The State of Theology* survey published in 2022, growing numbers of Americans in general (from 41 percent to 53 percent) and of evangelicals in particular (from 17 percent to 26 percent) believe that "the Bible, like all sacred writing, contains helpful accounts of ancient myths but is not literally true."[3] Given these beliefs, it is hardly surprising that immorality of all kinds also seems to be on the rise. *The State of Theology* documents this as well. For example, when asked whether "the Bible's condemnation of homosexual behavior" still applies today, fewer Americans and fewer evangelicals say yes. According to the prevailing cultural logic, if we do not believe that what God says is true, then we do not have to do what he says.

3　"The State of Theology," Ligonier Ministries, *thestateoftheology.com*, accessed October 17, 2022.

We have so much to learn by looking carefully at the dialogue in Genesis 3. From the story of naive Eve and the sly serpent, we learn that when doubts arise, the person who is most desperate for us to disbelieve the truth of God's word—including, perhaps, the truth of his own existence—is the devil. We learn that when doubts are dishonest—when, for example, we are not genuinely open to changing our minds about God—they usually have disobedience somewhere on their agenda. We also learn that when doubt expresses itself as disobedience—as it sometimes (but not always) does—we are headed for destruction. Eating the forbidden fruit did indeed lead to death, just as God said.

When We Have Doubts of Our Own

If we are honest, we have to admit that what happened to Eve is a temptation for us as well. Sometimes we have our doubts about the stories we read in the word of God, about its moral convictions and the promises it makes.

We know how truly human the Bible is, and we wonder if it is also fully divine. We question whether Adam and Eve were the parents of the entire human race. Can we square biblical teaching with scientific evidence? Our culture struggles with the Bible's sexual ethics, and maybe we do as well: two sexes, two genders, and one definition of marriage, in which a man and a woman are united in a lifelong covenant. Is the Bible right about the sanctity of life inside and outside the womb? Is it for or against women? Does it have a righteous view of justice, including racial justice? Does it give us a true perspective on the fundamental unity and the eternal diversity of humanity? Is it really true that our bodies will rise again and that we will all stand before God's throne for judgment?

In the face of such questions and objections, many skeptics believe (!) that the Bible is "scientifically impossible, historically unreliable, and culturally regressive."[4] Most of us can relate. If we read the Bible carefully, eventually we encounter something we find hard to accept, and maybe difficult to believe at all. The question is this: What should we do when this happens?

By way of answer, here are several practical steps we can take to give us growing confidence in the word of God.

First, we can *confess that we are not neutral observers* but are predisposed *not* to believe what God says. This is one of the sad results of humanity's first, morally fatal transgression. As soon as Adam and Eve ate the forbidden fruit, they hid from God—a clear sign that they were no longer aligned with his divine holiness. God called to Adam and said, "Where are you?" (Gen. 3:9). This showed that the first man had ended up far from God. Adam's sin has *noetic* effects on all of us; in other words, it distorts our spiritual ability to reason. Spiritual doubt comes more naturally to the fallen human heart than genuine faith does. Missiologist Lesslie Newbigin reminds us: "We are not honest inquirers seeking the truth. We are alienated from truth and are enemies of it."[5] If this is true, then we need to doubt our doubts and stay skeptical about our skepticism.

Second, we can *keep studying the Scriptures.* When we do, we will find out how reliable they are. The Bible is easily the best-attested text from the ancient world. We have—by far—more

---

4   Timothy Keller, *The Reason for God: Belief in an Age of Skepticism* (New York: Dutton, 2008), 99–100.

5   Lesslie Newbigin, *Proper Confidence: Faith, Doubt, and Certainty in Christian Disciple-ship* (Grand Rapids, MI: Eerdmans, 1995), 69.

well-preserved manuscripts of the Scriptures of the Old and New Testaments than we do of any other history book or sacred text from antiquity. We know what the Bible says.

Furthermore, the general trajectory of biblical scholarship is to confirm rather than to deny biblical history. To cite one notable example, some scholars used to cast doubt on the historicity of David, despite all the biblical evidence to the contrary. Those aspersions were set aside for good when archaeologists discovered a stone artifact at Tel Dan in 1993 and saw "the house of David" among its inscriptions. This proved that David's reign was engraved in stone as well as written in Scripture. Or consider Luke's assertion that Jesus was born "when Quirinius was governor of Syria" (Luke 2:2). Certain scholars used to claim that Luke's timetable was inaccurate. But as more information became available, it turned out that Doctor Luke knew more than these scholars did about the governorship of Quirinius and his census-taking in the Roman world.[6]

When we have our doubts, we need to study the Bible more, not less. We need to open it up, not set it aside. The overall direction of biblical interpretation encourages us to keep searching for the answers, so that in time we too may come to a better understanding of the truth. If we are wise, we will accept the mysteries, wrestle with the difficulties, live with the questions, and wait for the answers while we keep studying the word of God.

---

6 For more on Quirinius, see Leon Morris, *The Gospel according to St. Luke: An Introduction and Commentary*, Tyndale New Testament Commentaries (Grand Rapids, MI: Eerdmans, 1974), 82–83, and Norval Geldenhuys, *The Gospel of Luke*, New International Commentary on the New Testament (Grand Rapids, MI: Eerdmans, 1951), 100.

Third, we can *recognize that the Bible contains the faithful ring of truth*. When we have our doubts, it is easy to focus so much on what we think are problems that we miss the unmistakable signs of authenticity.

There are many things we would never expect to see in the Bible unless they were true. For example, we would not expect so many heroes of the faith—nearly all of them, in fact—to expose so many of their failings in its pages. It is really difficult to imagine an important leader like Peter coming off so badly in the church's sacred texts unless he himself had insisted on its accurate record of his ignorance, cowardice, and betrayal.[7] The best explanation for this unrivalled candor is that the authors of Scripture were telling the truth about themselves because they wanted us to know the truth about the mercy and grace that God showed them.

We could say something similar about Jesus of Nazareth—not about his sins, of course, because he committed no sin, but about some of the troubling facts in his biography. Why would the Bible ever speak of his spiritual struggle in the garden of Gethsemane, or proclaim that he was crucified as a common criminal, or record his words of dereliction from the cross unless these things actually happened? Even if we still have our doubts about certain parts of Scripture, we should recognize that its primary historical claims are true beyond any reasonable objection.

C. S. Lewis found a realism and attention to detail in the Bible that was unlike anything else in the literature of the ancient world, and this convinced him that its writers were telling the truth. Lewis wrote:

---

7 Richard Bauckham, *Jesus and the Eyewitnesses: The Gospels as Eyewitness Testimony* (Grand Rapids, MI: Eerdmans, 2006), 170–78, cited in Keller, *The Reason for God*, 105.

I have been reading poems, romances, vision literature, legends, and myths all my life. I know what they are like. I know none of them are like this. Of this text there are only two possible views. Either this is reportage . . . or else, some unknown writer . . . without known predecessors or successors, suddenly anticipated the whole technique of modern novelistic, realistic narrative.[8]

Fourth, we can *do what the Bible says*, which of course is a lifelong challenge for us all. Some doubters and skeptics want to determine whether the Bible is true first, and *then* perhaps they will start to obey its teachings. But the first thing Jesus said to Andrew, Peter, and the other disciples was "Follow me!" (Matt. 4:19). Then he sat down to teach them what they needed to know (see Matt. 5:2ff.). Doing and believing go together. Indeed, we do not truly believe in Jesus unless and until we begin to follow him. The longer I live, the truer the Bible gets, not only because I get answers to all my questions but also because I have tested its truth through a lifetime of faith. We learn the hope and beauty of the Bible by living into its teachings.

Fifth, we can *pray for the help of the Holy Spirit*. We need God's help to believe God's word. One of the most important claims the Bible makes about itself is that it was "breathed out" by God the Holy Spirit (2 Tim. 3:16; cf. 2 Pet. 1:21). The Spirit of God is not a subjective feeling but a living, supernatural person—someone who has the divine power to confirm our minds and hearts in the truth of Scripture. John Calvin wrote beautifully about the Spirit's work in his famous *Institutes*:

8   C. S. Lewis, *Christian Reflections*, ed. Walter Hooper (Grand Rapids, MI: Eerdmans, 1967), 155.

The testimony of the Spirit is more excellent than all reason. For as God alone is a fit witness of himself in his Word, so also the Word will not find acceptance in man's heart before it is sealed by the inward testimony of the Spirit. The same Spirit, therefore, who has spoken through the mouths of the prophets must penetrate into our hearts to persuade us that they faithfully proclaimed what had been divinely commanded.[9]

Sixth, if we are having our doubts about the Bible, we can *refuse to give up too soon*. I say this partly because our eternal destiny depends on it. Only the Scriptures are able to make us "wise for salvation through faith in Christ Jesus" (2 Tim. 3:15). But I say it even more because I know that God wants to bless us with growing faith that leads to full assurance. He wants to answer for us the same prayer that the apostle Paul offered on behalf of the Colossians, that our "hearts may be encouraged . . . to reach all the riches of full assurance of understanding and the knowledge of God's mystery, which is Christ" (Col. 2:2).

When by the grace of God we experience full confidence in the word of God, we are able to testify to its complete reliability and eternally saving power. "The Bible can be trusted," writes Timothy George, "to be totally reliable on its own terms: its history is historical and its miracles are miraculous, and its theology is God's own truth."[10]

---

9   John Calvin, *Institutes of the Christian Religion*, ed. John T. McNeill, trans. Ford Lewis Battles, 2 vols., Library of Christian Classics 20–21 (Philadelphia: Westminster, 1960), 1.7.4.

10   Timothy George, "What We Mean When We Say It's True," *Christianity Today*, October 23, 1995, https://www.christianitytoday.com/.

A Step of Faith

Notice that I have not offered any kind of proof. According to Lesslie Newbigin, "There can be no indubitable proofs"; the only two "possible responses to the claims that the Bible makes are belief or unbelief."[11] That is mainly because of the kind of book the Bible is. Although it makes many truth claims, it is not a compendium of logical propositions. Instead, it is the true story of a relationship that God invites us to make our own. Because our story is still being written, we must trust the faithful Author to make it come out right in the end. Our only certainty, then, is "the certainty of *faith*."[12]

The kind of knowledge we should expect from the Bible is the same kind of knowing we experience in our relationships. "In this kind of knowing," Newbigin writes, "we are not in full control. We may ask questions, but we must also answer the questions put by the other."[13] There is give and take. There is also room to grow. We can ask God all the questions we like, but we cannot hold him at arm's length, as if he were simply the object of our scrutiny. We have questions for him, but he also has questions for us—questions such as "Where were you when I laid the foundation of the earth?" (Job 38:4) or "Who do you say that I am?" (Matt. 16:15) or "Whom shall I send, and who will go for us?" (Isa. 6:8).

A sculpture on the campus of Wheaton College makes a dramatic statement about our dynamic relationship with Scripture.

11 Newbigin, *Proper Confidence*, 55.

12 Keith Johnson, "Doubt," in *Life Questions Every Student Asks: Faithful Responses to Common Issues*, ed. Gary M. Burge and David Lauber (Downers Grove, IL: InterVarsity Press, 2020), 135, emphasis original.

13 Newbigin, *Proper Confidence*, 10.

The sculpture is a large bronze book—about three feet high—with layers upon layers of open pages. The artist, Liviu Mocan, gave his work the provocative title *The Book That Reads You*. The sculptor's point is that while we are reading the Bible, it is also reading us, discerning our desires and our commitments. How will we respond? This is a much more important question than any of the questions we have about the Bible. We are inside the story, not outside of it, and sooner or later we all have to make a choice: Will I trust the God of the Bible or not?

Billy Graham made his decision at Forest Home—a Christian retreat center in California. At the time, the young preacher was questioning his calling as an evangelist and wrestling with the hard questions people asked him about the truth of Scripture. Seeking definitive answers, he went out into the woods alone, set his Bible on a stump, and started to pray:

> O God! There are many things in this book I do not understand. There are many problems with it for which I have no solution. There are many seeming contradictions. There are some areas in it that do not seem to correlate with modern science. I can't answer some of the philosophical and psychological questions [people] are raising.

Then the brilliant evangelist fell to his knees and declared, "Father, I am going to accept this as Thy Word—by faith! I'm going to allow faith to go beyond my intellectual questions and doubts, and I will believe this to be Your inspired Word."[14]

---

14 Will Graham, "The Tree Stump Prayer: When Billy Graham Overcame Doubt," Billy Graham Evangelistic Association, July 9, 2014, https://billygraham.org/.

Graham preached at the campground that night with fresh authority; more than four hundred people gave their lives to Jesus Christ. Just a few weeks later he began his Los Angeles Crusade, which touched the nation. Many years later he testified:

> I've discovered something in my ministry: When I take the Bible literally, when I proclaim it as the word of God, my preaching has power. When I stand on the platform and say, "God says," or "The Bible says," the Holy Spirit uses me. There are results. Wiser men than you or I have been arguing questions like this for centuries. I don't have the time or the intellect to examine all sides of the theological dispute, so I've decided once for all to stop questioning and accept the Bible as God's word.[15]

Sadly, Billy Graham knew a fellow evangelist who made exactly the opposite decision. The man's name was Charles Templeton. The two preachers toured Europe together in 1946, proclaiming the gospel. But Templeton started to have his doubts, and by 1957 he had publicly de-converted from Christianity. "Billy," he said, "it's simply not possible any longer to believe." Templeton first became an agnostic and then later a well-known apologist for atheism. When he was interviewed about his religious views near the end of his life, he said wistfully, "Everything good I know, everything decent I know, everything pure I know, I learned from Jesus." Templeton wept openly after he said this, but then dismissed any further conversation about spiritual matters with the words "Enough of that!"[16]

---

15 Billy Graham, quoted in Justin Taylor, "Charles Templeton: Missing Jesus," TGC, May 9, 2013, https://www.thegospelcoalition.org/.

16 Templeton's tragic spiritual journey is outlined in Taylor, "Charles Templeton."

Our Mother in the Faith

Everyone has to make choices and then live with the consequences, whether tragic or triumphant. Our mother Eve made her choice in the difficult years that followed the loss of paradise. While I regret her transgression as much as anything, I also admire her subsequent life of faith as "the mother of all living" (Gen. 3:20).

Eve stood by Adam's side as the two of them heard the first promise of the gospel: a son that would crush the serpent's head (Gen. 3:15). Eve believed it because God said it. She also received the first sign of salvation: the animal skins that covered her shame (Gen. 3:21). Evidently, she believed the good news as much as she could, because when her first son was born, Eve declared, "I have gotten a man with the help of the LORD" (Gen. 4:1). Martin Luther preferred an alternative translation: "I have brought forth the God-man."[17] As it turned out, that child was not the Son of God incarnate—only another sinner. But Eve was believing into the promise of God that a Savior would come, as eventually he did. We should not think of our first mother merely as a sinner and a doubter. Remember instead that she was the first believer!

We imitate Eve's life of faith when we take God at his word and trust his promise for our own salvation in Jesus Christ by his sin-defeating death and life-giving resurrection. If anyone tries to tempt us with a question that begins with the words "Did God *actually* say . . . ," we will interrupt as politely as we can, point to something specific in the Bible, and say, "Yes, as a matter of fact, he did!"

---

17 See Jonathan Black, "Eve Was a Christian," *Apostolic Theology*, July 22, 2014, https://www.apostolictheology.org/.

*The L*ORD *said to Abraham, "Why did Sarah laugh*
and say, 'Shall I indeed bear a child, now that
*I am old?' Is anything too hard for the L*ORD*?"*

GENESIS 18:13–14

2

Doubting God's Saving Promise

Sarah under the Oak Trees

WHEN MY CHILDREN WERE SMALL, they often asked whether they could do this or have that. My standard response was "We'll see"—an answer that didn't mean no, necessarily, but didn't mean yes, either. My purpose was to teach my sons and daughters that they could count on their father's word. If I wasn't certain enough to make a commitment, I would rather give my children the mild disappointment of uncertainty than to make a promise I wasn't totally sure I could keep. If I said, "Yes, you can have that" or "I promise we'll do it," they would have the security of my paternal word. A promise made should be a promise kept.

This principle explains why I was so disappointed one day when I saw a "Closed" sign on Philadelphia's Civil War Museum. I had told my daughter Kirsten that I would take her there to see the mounted head of Old Baldy—the famous horse that General George G. Meade rode at the Battle of Gettysburg. It seemed like a safe promise: we walked by the museum in Center City Philadelphia every week on our way to church. Yet, suddenly and inexplicably the museum closed. When I discovered that the closure was permanent, I realized that I had done something I had told myself I would never do: make a promise to one of my children that I wouldn't be able to keep. Eventually, Kirsten and I agreed on an alternative outing and all was forgiven, but to this day, I still don't feel good about it. A father should keep his word!

This principle lies at the heart of our faith. Our Father in heaven has promises to keep, and thankfully he is committed to keeping them. When we begin to doubt this—as sometimes we do—we lose the assurance of our salvation and the confidence to live with Christian courage.

Why Sarah Laughed

The biblical story of Sarah under the oak trees is about doubting God's promises. One very hot day, Sarah's husband, Abraham, was sitting at the door of their tent, sheltered under a stand of oak trees. He was surprised to see three men appear suddenly before him. Abraham bowed to greet them and then welcomed them according to ancient custom, with a lavish meal. As the visitors washed their feet and cooled off under the tall trees, Sarah baked some bread while Abraham killed a fattened calf, prepared the meat, and brought it to his guests with milk and cheese.

The most important thing to know about Abraham is that God had given him some very precious promises. God had told Abraham that he would become "the father of a multitude of nations" (Gen. 17:5)—that through him "all the families of the earth" would be blessed (Gen. 12:3).

God made these lavish promises and then took his own sweet time to fulfill them. In fact, by the time of Genesis 18, he hadn't yet kept his word at all. The years passed—Abraham turned seventy, eighty, ninety-nine. His wife, Sarah, wasn't getting any younger, either; she had celebrated her eighty-ninth birthday. Still, the old couple had no child to call their own. Humanly speaking, it seemed certain that they would die before they saw God fulfill the main promises he had made to them.

This is the backstory for the conversation that took place outside Abraham's tent. The visitors were angels, and when they spoke, they brought Abraham a message from God. First, they inquired, "Where is Sarah your wife?" (v. 9). Abraham said she was inside the tent, and their spokesman responded with a simple promise: "I will surely return to you about this time next year, and Sarah your wife shall have a son" (v. 10).

This set up a dramatic moment in the history of salvation. Sarah had been "listening at the tent door" (v. 10). She was so old, the Bible tells us, that "the way of women had ceased to be" with her (v. 11). To put it bluntly, she had been through menopause and there was not a chance on earth she would *ever* give birth now. So, when a stranger came and said that she would experience childbirth and become a mother, "Sarah laughed to herself" and said, "After I am worn out, and my lord is old, shall I have pleasure?" (v. 12).

Make no mistake: Sarah knew that this was God's promise. The Bible clues us in to this by referring to one of the messengers as "the LORD" himself (vv. 10, 13). But Sarah had also heard this promise before, that God would make her husband the father of many nations. She had prayed for God to fulfill this promise. When intercession didn't work, she blamed God for failing to keep his word. A few chapters earlier she said, "Behold now, the Lord has prevented me from bearing children" (Gen. 16:2). Then Sarah infamously came up with another way to have a son. She offered her servant to her husband as a surrogate (Gen. 16:3)—with consequences that were far from fortunate.

These actions and interactions show how central the promise of a son had been to Sarah's life experience. It would have been wisest for her to wait upon God for the fulfillment of his promise. But waiting on God requires, as Elisabeth Elliot has written, "the willingness to bear uncertainty, to carry within oneself the unanswered question, lifting the heart to God about it whenever it intrudes upon one's thoughts."[1] Such prayerful surrender to God's purposes was precisely Sarah's struggle.

After everything that had happened—and everything that *didn't* happen—we can understand why Sarah laughed when she overheard someone say that she would conceive and bear a son. It wasn't a merry laugh, either. It had an edge to it. Her sarcastic words—"after I am worn out, . . . shall I have pleasure?" (Gen. 18:12)—reveal the doubts of a heart that was hardening against God.

Recognize everything that Sarah doubted. She doubted God's goodness. She doubted the truth of God's word. She doubted that he cared very much about her situation. She doubted that he would answer her prayers. Most basically of all, she doubted that God would ever make good on the salvation he promised to

---

1 Elisabeth Elliot, *Passion and Purity: Learning to Bring Your Love Life under Christ's Control* (Grand Rapids, MI: Revell, 2006), 61–62.

his people. Sarah's spiritual experience made her skeptical about nearly everything she had heard about God—everything he had promised to his people.

Sarah is not alone. Most of us have life experiences that beget spiritual doubts and perhaps sarcasm about biblical Christianity. We didn't get what we hoped and prayed for, even if it seemed to be something good and godly. As far as we could tell, God hardly seemed to notice when we were struggling. Some of the things we were led to expect when we committed our lives to Christ never really happened. We found ourselves struggling with the same old problems, or still waiting for God to answer a prayer that eventually we gave up making because it was too discouraging to keep asking without ever getting an answer. We ended up feeling like the world-weary psalmist, who asked:

> Will the Lord spurn forever,
>   and never again be favorable?
> Has his steadfast love forever ceased?
>   Are his promises at an end for all time? (Ps. 77:7–8)

Some of our doubts are as deep as Sarah's: they are about the core promises of salvation. John Calvin said that the main reason we doubt is that our "circumstances are all in opposition to the promises of God. He promises us immortality; yet we are surrounded by mortality and corruption. He declares that he accounts us just; yet we are covered with sins."[2] We could easily

---

2 John Calvin, *Calvin's Commentary: The Epistles of Paul to the Romans and to the Thessalonians*, trans. Ross McKenzie, ed. David W. Torrance and Thomas F. Torrance (Grand Rapids, MI: Eerdmans, 1994), 99, quoted in Keith Johnson, "Doubt," in *Life*

add to Calvin's list. God has promised to be with us, but we feel all alone. God has promised to make us holy, but we struggle so hard with sin that we doubt we will ever be pure. God has promised to raise us up to everlasting life, but there are days when that seems improbable, if not impossible. When we die, will we really live again?

Sometimes it is easier to doubt than to believe—especially when it comes to God's eternal, supernatural promises. This is confirmed by social research from the people who began the "He Gets Us" marketing campaign in 2022. Their evangelistic advertisements started with phrases like "Jesus hated politics, too" and "A rebel took to the streets—he recruited others to join him." These commercials tried to connect with ordinary people by emphasizing our Savior's humanity. This is a good way to start a spiritual conversation, because most Americans accept the Jesus of history. Unfortunately, as soon as we start talking as well about the *divinity* of Jesus, people start to have their doubts. Yet there is no Christianity without a Christ who is God as well as man. Therefore, in faithfully communicating the gospel we must address the supernatural promises of God.

Calling Out Doubt

Anyone who has trouble accepting the miraculous aspects of the Christian faith should see how Sarah's story continues—not just for her but for the whole wide world.

Before Sarah became a believer—which eventually she did—God called her out for being a doubter. This was important

---

Questions Every Student Asks: Faithful Responses to Common Issues, ed. Gary M. Burge and David Lauber (Downers Grove, IL: InterVarsity Press, 2020), 133–34.

because it clarified her spiritual condition. Rather than letting her drift along somewhere between faith and unbelief without making a clear spiritual commitment, the Lord confronted Sarah's skepticism. He said to Abraham, "Why did Sarah laugh and say, 'Shall I indeed bear a child, now that I am old?'" (Gen. 18:13). Sarah did what people usually do when they are caught in a compromising position: she "denied it, saying, 'I did not laugh,'" for she was afraid." This was a lie, and thankfully the Lord refused to let her get away with it. "No, but you did laugh," he said (Gen. 18:15).

The Lord knew *exactly* what Sarah did and did not believe. When she was alone in her tent, scoffing at the hope of bearing a child, God not only heard her laughter but also knew what it meant. Sarah did not believe God's promise that she would conceive and bear a son. We know this from what the angel said to her next: "Is anything too hard for the LORD? At the appointed time I will return to you, about this time next year, and Sarah shall have a son" (Gen. 18:14). Simply put, Sarah only believed in what seemed possible, not what seemed impossible. She had not yet learned that with God, *nothing* is impossible. So she doubted.

Wherever we stand with respect to the promises of God—and whatever we do or don't believe about God, the Bible, and salvation—the Holy Spirit knows all about it. If we are strong in hope, God sees our faith and will call us to depend even more upon his promises. But if we have our doubts—whether big or small—our skepticism is hardly a secret. Our dubious criticism of biblical truth, the unkind comment we've made about someone else's spiritual zeal, the private curse we've uttered when something hasn't gone our way—the Holy Spirit always knows all about it.

Far from wanting to cover up these skeptical doubts and sarcastic comments, God wants to bring them out into the open. In fact, he would like to do for us what he did for Sarah and clarify what we *don't* believe so that in time he can turn us into sincere believers. Sarah did not believe that God would keep his promise. Bringing that secret doubt into the light of day was an important step in her coming to faith. In fact, in the end Sarah's doubts made her a stronger believer. Her story thus encourages us to keep fighting for our faith. By the mercy of God, one day we will get "the benefit of the doubt," which is strong assurance of our faith.

The Prequel and the Sequel

To see how Sarah came to faith, we need to look both backward and forward, because what happened to Sarah under the oak trees has both a prequel and a sequel.

The prequel took place in the garden of Eden. Genesis is written in a form that helps us see connections between Sarah and Eve, her mother in the faith. There are striking similarities. Both stories took place near a tree, and both involve deception. In both stories someone is concealed from God. Remember how Eve and Adam tried to hide from God as a way of covering up their sin? In both stories, God asks some pointed questions, even though he knows exactly what has happened before asking. Both stories include the promise of a blessed birth: the serpent crusher in Genesis 3:15 and the nation builder in Genesis 18. The word *eden* shows up in both stories too, although it is hard to spot in English. When Sarah asks doubtfully whether she will experience the joy of motherhood in Genesis 18:12, the word she uses for "pleasure" is a form of the word *eden*.

Why does the Bible make all these connections? To show us that God is starting to make good on his promise of reversing the curse. The first promise of the gospel was that a woman would give birth to a son who would bring salvation. That blessed promise was repeated to Sarah and Abraham. Even if Sarah had trouble believing it at first, that promise was starting to come true. These stories are told to show us that something much bigger is happening than simply a surprising birth announcement. God is working his saving plan.

We see one fulfillment of the promise in Genesis 21, when Sarah gives birth to her firstborn son. The Bible says, "The Lord visited Sarah as he had said, and the Lord did to Sarah as he had promised" (v. 1). The point is repeated for emphasis: God did what he said *and* made good on what he promised. So it was that "Sarah conceived and bore Abraham a son in his old age at the time of which God had spoken to him" (vv. 1–2). Sarah's son was the proof. At first, she didn't believe, but by the time she held her baby in her arms, there was no way she could doubt any longer: God did as he promised.

There is a sequel too—the one we read in the opening chapters of the Gospel of Luke, where another old couple is unexpectedly expecting: Zechariah and Elizabeth. They too are long past their childbearing years. Nevertheless, a child is born; a son is given. The happy couple call him John the Baptist. He is the forerunner for an even more astonishing announcement. A shining angel visits a virgin girl in the lake country with a life-changing, world-saving declamation:

> Do not be afraid, Mary, for you have found favor with God. And behold, you will conceive in your womb and bear a son, and you shall call his name Jesus. He will be great and will be called the Son of the Most High. And the Lord God will give to him the throne of his father David, and he will reign over the house of Jacob forever, and of his kingdom there will be no end. (Luke 1:30–33)

What happened to Sarah and Elizabeth was merely improbable—a maternal marvel. But what happened to Mary was truly impossible—something only God the Holy Spirit could do. The ancient prophecy was fulfilled, first in Nazareth and then in Bethlehem. A *virgin* did conceive and bear a son, as Isaiah had prophesied (Isa. 7:14). A virgin! In her Christmas picture book for children, Madeleine L'Engle rightly calls this birth *The Glorious Impossible*.[3] He was the Son of God, incarnate.

When the angel came and told Mary something she could hardly believe, Mary asked an honest question: How could this happen? The angel's answer was simple: "The Holy Spirit will come upon you, and the power of the Most High will overshadow you; therefore the child to be born will be called holy—the Son of God" (Luke 1:35). This was all that Mary needed to hear. She didn't doubt; she believed. She didn't laugh; she worshiped. She didn't resist; she surrendered. Her faith-filled response—"Let it

---

3 Madeleine L'Engle, *The Glorious Impossible: Illustrated with Frescoes from the Scrovegni Chapel by Giotto* (New York: Simon & Schuster, 1990).

be to me according to your word" (Luke 1:38)—is a model and an inspiration for every believer.

When we read Mary's story carefully, we may notice an important connection back to Sarah's story—a connection that helps us put our own doubts in their full biblical context. The angel in Sarah's story raised a rhetorical question: "Is anything too hard for the LORD?" (Gen. 18:14). The implied answer, of course, is "No, nothing is too hard for God." The angel in Mary's story uses nearly the same words as Moses did but puts them in the form of a declaration that properly ends with an exclamation mark rather than a question mark: "For nothing will be impossible with God" (Luke 1:37)!

Here is a principle for us to live by. We serve the God of the impossible, who is able "to do far more abundantly than all that we ask or think" (Eph. 3:20). Do we believe this?

Justin Skeesuck and Patrick Gray tested their faith in God's possible by taking an improbable journey across five hundred miles of the mountainous trail that winds across France and Spain before leading pilgrims to the cathedral of Santiago de Compostela in Galicia.[4] Skeesuck has a neuromuscular disease that confines him to a wheelchair, so essentially his best friend had to push, drag, and carry him across the trail, mile by rugged mile. In the first hours of their springtime journey, when Skeesuck's wheelchair repeatedly got stuck in the mud, a local man ran to tell them that what they were doing was impossible. However, when it became clear that the two friends were determined to make this pilgrimage regardless, the man gave them a blessing that lifted their spirits

---

4 The two friends tell their story in Patrick Gray and Justin Skeesuck, *I'll Push You: A Journey of 500 Miles, Two Best Friends, and One Wheelchair* (Wheaton, IL: Tyndale, 2017).

and served as a rallying cry for the rest of their journey: "With God, the impossible is possible!"

Like Justin and Patrick—as well as Sarah and Mary—we will discover how much is possible for God when we venture out in faith and trust him to keep his promises every step of the way. Christian Wiman challenges us all to greater boldness on our spiritual journey when he writes, "What we call doubt is often simply dullness of mind and spirit, not the absence of faith at all, but faith latent in the lives we are not quite living, God dormant in the world to which we are not quite giving our best selves."[5]

The Last Laugh

Three mothers, three miracle babies, and one story of salvation in Jesus Christ. Obviously, of these three women, Mary is the best model for our faith. She was not a doubter or a deceiver but a humble, faithful believer.

We shouldn't be too hard on Sarah, however, because although she doubted at first, eventually she became a stronger believer because of it. The book of Hebrews puts her on the famous list in chapter 11—the Faith Hall of Fame—where we read that "by faith Sarah herself received power to conceive, even when she was past the age, since she considered him faithful who had promised" (v. 11). This brief explanation assures us that Sarah believed God's purpose even before her baby was born.

The name that Sarah gave her newborn son is another confirmation of the faith that conquered her doubts. She called him Isaac, which is the Hebrew word for "laughter." By way of explanation,

---

5   Christian Wiman, *My Bright Abyss: Meditation of a Modern Believer* (New York: Farrar, Straus and Giroux, 2013), 77.

she said: "God has made laughter for me; everyone who hears will laugh over me. . . . Who would have said to Abraham that Sarah would nurse children? Yet I have borne him a son in his old age" (Gen. 21:6–7).

By calling to mind Sarah's faithless, uncontrollable laughter when the angel told her husband that they would conceive and bear a son, these words prove that Sarah was able to laugh at herself, which, after all, is one of the clearest signs of spiritual and emotional health. Sarah invited other people to laugh at her too. When her baby was born, she realized how humorous it was that she had ever doubted the power and the promises of God. So she gave her one and only son a name that would remind everyone how she had once scoffed at the very idea that she could still have a son.

I imagine Sarah laughing her way through the rest of her earthly days. Imagine how happy she must have been when she realized that God was starting to fulfill his promise. Did she smile the night that she and Abraham made love? Did she chuckle the first time she realized that the reason she had been so irritable was her morning sickness? Could she help but laugh the first time she felt a little swish inside her and realized that new life was moving in her womb?

What we know for certain is that Sarah laughed out loud when her child was born, her son was given. This time her laughter was not bitter and sarcastic, the way it was when she was hiding from God, but joyous and holy. When God proved himself to Sarah, it brought new joy into her life. One of the differences between faith and unbelief is the way we laugh—either as an expression of mockery or else as a form of worship. The deepest laughter comes from the enduring surprise of knowing that God graciously keeps all his promises.

How will God prove himself to us? And how will we respond? God proved himself to Sarah by seeing her situation, promising her a blessing, and then delivering on his promise. According to Herman Bavinck, God the Holy Spirit wants to prove himself to every one of us by meeting us in a personal way. Bavinck writes:

> Holy Scripture does not want to give us an abstract concept of deity, but rather wants to put us into contact, all of us personally, with the living and true God. Scripture breaks off our notions and concepts and leads us back to God Himself. Hence Scripture does not argue about God, but presents Him to us and shows Him in all the works of his hand.[6]

The most beautiful work of God's hand is salvation in Jesus Christ—from his incarnation in the virgin's womb, to his life of perfect obedience, to his message of repentance and faith, to his atoning sacrifice on the cross, to his triumphant resurrection from the grave, to his righteous judgment at the end of history. The Bible says that "no matter how many promises God has made, they are 'Yes' in Christ" (2 Cor. 1:20 NIV). When we behold the child in the manger, when we see the Christ on the cross, when we peer into the empty tomb, and when we see the glory of God in the face of Jesus Christ, we see God's yes to all the promises he ever made.

6 Herman Bavinck, *The Wonderful Works of God,* trans. Henry Zylstra (1956; repr., Philadelphia: Westminster Seminary Press, 2020), 144.

When we realize what this means for us—forgiveness, healing, loving care, future hope, eternal life—sometimes we just have to laugh. Doubters may scoff at the promises of God, but believers always get the last laugh. With Eve and Sarah and Mary—our mothers in the faith—we will spend the rest of eternity laughing with joy every time we remember our former doubts and realize again that God made good on every promise that he ever made to us in Jesus Christ.

But Moses said to God, "Who am I that I should go to Pharaoh and bring the children of Israel out of Egypt?"

EXODUS 3:11

3

Doubting God's Missional Call

Moses at the Burning Bush

BY NOW IT SHOULD BE CLEAR that this book is about living honestly with our doubts and honoring God in the way we hold them. It is about leaning into a life of faith when it is hard to believe and recognizing that doubt is a normal part of the Christian life. It is also about walking beside other pilgrims who struggle to believe what they know is true or to live with their questions while they are still looking for the answers. It is not primarily about trying to prove that God is there or solving the main problems in classical apologetics. Rather, it is about the full range of questions we have as Christians—all the doubts that trouble our souls as we try and sometimes fail to follow Jesus.

The best way to begin working through any spiritual struggle is to open the Bible and see what it says. When we study the Scriptures from the vantage point of faith and doubt, two things stand out. One is that almost everyone in the Bible who is known for his or her faith also struggled with unbelief. "Doubting Thomas," so-called, is not the only disciple who had trouble believing in Jesus. And at one point or another, all of the men and women we will meet in this book—Eve, Sarah, Jeremiah, Peter, and the rest—had their doubts.

We also learn from the Scriptures that people who bring their doubts before God find faith to move forward. They do not always have their questions answered. In fact, most of them are called to step out in faith *before* they get all the answers. They do not always stop doubting, either. The questions that came once come again. Or they are replaced by entirely new doubts that make it hard to trust and obey. And yet, by the grace of God, doubters do become believers, and also followers. Many of the strongest Christians prove to be men and women who were honest about their doubts, prayed through their questions, and were open to seeing what God wanted to show them.

When God Called Moses

Moses is a prime example of the doubter-believers we meet in the Bible. The man certainly had his doubts—specifically, about his ability to do what he knew perfectly well God was telling him to do. Moses is a man who doubted God's missional call.

Born a slave in Egypt, concealed and then rescued from the Nile in infancy, educated in the courts of Pharaoh—Moses knew the power and prestige that came with living in a place of privilege. But he also experienced total failure. Angered one day by the mistreatment of a fellow Hebrew, he struck and killed a slave driver. In effect, Moses tried to set his people free one Egyptian at a time. But instead of becoming a liberator, he was called a murderer and fled into the wilderness for forty years as a fugitive from justice.

There in the desert Moses met the living God. As he was out tending his flocks one day, he saw a burning bush that was not reduced to ashes but kept burning bright. The Lord spoke from this flaming bush, calling Moses by name. God told him to take off his sandals because he was standing on holy ground. Then the Lord gave a clear and unmistakable call: "Come, I will send you to Pharaoh that you may bring my people, the children of Israel, out of Egypt" (Ex. 3:10).

Many people wonder what they should do with their lives— where they should go to school, what they should study, whom they should marry, where they should live, what career path to follow, when to retire. Moses did not have this problem. Instead, he received what most people want, or think they want: a clear call from God. How could he possibly have any doubts? He was standing on holy ground, witnessing a fiery miracle, listening to God speak with an audible voice, hearing exactly where he should go and what he should say. There was no doubt about the presence of God or about what he was calling Moses to do.

Yet immediately Moses began to question the Almighty and even to bargain for a better deal. Basically, he doubted whether he was the right man for the job. In the conversation that followed, Moses expressed several querulous hesitations. He told God that he was too much of a nobody to appear before Pharaoh. He said that if he did go to Pharaoh (which he wasn't planning to do anyway; notice Ex. 3:13: "*If* I come to the people of Israel"), he wouldn't know what to say (although he never seemed to be at a loss for words when he was arguing with God!). Moses pointed out that he did not have the proper diplomatic credentials. He observed that if he tried to tell people that he was speaking for God, they would never believe him. He even claimed that he had received a failing grade in public speaking, or words to similar effect. So the conversation went. It was one objection after another.

Finally, Moses came right out and said, "Oh, my Lord, please send someone else" (Ex. 4:13). This was the exact opposite of what Isaiah said when God called him to go and preach the gospel. Isaiah said: "Here I am! Send me" (Isa. 6:8). But when God called Moses from the burning bush, although at first he said, "Here I am" (Ex. 3:4), once he knew what God wanted him to do, he basically said, "Send anyone else *but* me."

Many of us can relate. Do I have what it takes? Will I measure up, or will I come up short—spiritually, intellectually, musically, athletically, aesthetically, socially, professionally, or otherwise? Is this where I belong? Can I really do what I sense God is calling me to do? It is easy to feel overwhelmed and hard to believe that we will achieve our goals, find the love and respect we desire, or fulfill God's purpose for our lives. We all have our doubts.

What the Real Doubt Was

Based on what Moses said, we might think that his doubts were mainly about himself. After all, his complaints seem to focus on his own abilities, or lack thereof. Obviously, the man was plagued by self-doubt.

Or was he? To understand this story and its implications for our own sacred callings, we need to recognize that whatever doubts Moses had were really about God and not about himself. We know this from the way God answered him. God did not tell Moses to have more confidence in his own abilities. He did not say that his past mistakes would prepare him for future success. He did not try to convince him that he had the educational background and the intellectual ability to hold his own in Pharaoh's court, or that he was a better orator than he thought he was.

Sometimes we say similar things to ourselves, and in the end we are no more reassured than Moses was: "You've got the ability." "You've learned your lessons and now it's time to put them into practice." "You're well prepared." "You're more talented than you think you are." "God won't ever give you more than you can handle." These platitudes may be true, as far as they go. But they will not be very reassuring when life turns out to be harder than we expected, or when we meet people with far more ability than we have, or when God gives us far more than anyone but he can handle.

When we focus on ourselves, our self-doubts get bigger, not smaller. This is why God did not encourage Moses to think about himself at all, but called the man to trust in God instead. At every turning point in this long debate at the burning bush, God pointed Moses away from himself and back to the loving grace and mighty power of his living Lord.

Their conversation went something like this: After God called Moses by name, he identified himself as "the God of your father, the God of Abraham, the God of Isaac, and the God of Jacob" (Ex. 3:6). Rather than encouraging Moses to look back at his own track record, God invited the man to recognize his divine faithfulness from generation to generation. We have the same assurance. God is not just our God; he is the God of our fathers and mothers in the faith. He has been there for his people in the past. He sees us today the way he saw the children of Israel when they were slaves in Egypt, and he has a plan to deliver us from all our troubles, too. Jesus has given us this promise: "I will never leave you nor forsake you" (Heb. 13:5).

When Moses proceeded to object that he did not have the credibility to appear before Pharaoh, God ignored the man's résumé completely and said, "But I will be with you" (Ex. 3:12). It didn't matter who Moses was or what he had accomplished. Nor does it matter who we are or what we have done in the past. What matters is who God is, and what he can do!

Next, Moses claimed that the Israelites wouldn't listen to him any more than Pharaoh would. This was truly impertinent, because God had told him already that the Israelites *would* listen to him (Ex. 3:18). *But what if they don't?* Moses wondered. In response, God brought the conversation right back to the main point, which was his own eternal existence, constant presence, and almighty power. If anyone wants to know who sent you, God said to Moses, tell them this: "I AM WHO I AM. . . . I AM has sent me to you" (Ex. 3:14). God was saying it again: this was not about Moses, with all his hesitations and limitations. Instead, it was about the preexistent, self-existent, everlasting God—the God who cannot be consumed—the same God who has revealed himself to us in Jesus Christ as the great "I am."[1] This great God would be everything that his people needed him to be.

The problem—as Moses perceived it—was that he was all alone at the burning bush, and therefore no one else would believe him when he said that he had met with the living God. They

---

1   See John 6:35; 8:12; 10:9, 11; 11:25; 14:6; 15:1.

too would have their doubts. "They will not believe me or listen to my voice," Moses said. They will say, dismissively, "The Lord did not appear to you" (Ex. 4:1). How would anyone know that God really did appear to Moses, or that he said whatever Moses claimed he had said?

So it was that Moses dared to ask God for a sign. God generously gave him not one but three miraculous signs: a staff that became a serpent and then became a staff again; a cloak that turned his hand snow white with leprosy and then made his skin clean and healthy again; and—in case they didn't believe either of those two extraordinary signs—water from the Nile that turned into blood.

Three miracles should have been more than enough. But Moses kept thinking about all his limitations and tried a new line of attack. He said, "Oh, my Lord, I am not eloquent, either in the past or since you have spoken to your servant, but I am slow of speech and of tongue" (Ex. 4:10). Most people can relate. This is not because we have a speech impediment, feel inarticulate, or have a bad case of glossophobia (the fear of public speaking), which is estimated to afflict up to 75 percent of all Americans. We can relate because we too have doubts that never seem to end. If we keep focusing on ourselves, we will always find one more flaw to criticize, one more reason to hold back, one more problem no one else can solve, another doubt to undermine our faith. The more we look at ourselves, the more we get down on ourselves, as Moses did. The self-doubts—which are really God-doubts—never end.

Once again, God had the answer. Rather than admitting that Moses was right and conceding that he would need to find someone more qualified to do his kingdom work, God asserted his claim on Moses as his Creator: "Who has made man's mouth?

Who makes him mute, or deaf, or seeing, or blind? Is it not I, the LORD? Now therefore go, and I will be with your mouth and teach you what you shall speak" (Ex. 4:11–12).

God didn't back down on his calling for Moses but kept sending him to be his servant. Whatever the man's natural abilities, liabilities, or disabilities may have been, all of them were God given. God made Moses—he made us all—just the way he intended. His missional call on our lives takes everything into account. If we keep doubting whether God has a purpose for us, therefore, or questioning whether we are able to answer God's call, we are not really doubting ourselves but the God who created us just the way he wanted us to be.

At the point when God's calling for us is clear, our honest doubts are in perilous danger of becoming disrespectful and therefore sinful. Barnabas Piper cautions: "Often the intellectual obstacle to belief is a convenient excuse for rebellion. So when we ask we must desire to both hear the answer and *accept* the answer."[2] It is important for us to recognize, therefore, when our self-doubts are really God-doubts: "I'm not beautiful." "I'm not acceptable." "I'm not good enough or godly enough." "I'm not equal to the task that God has given me." If that is what we think, then we need to know that our heavenly Father made us in his own beautiful image, that we are forgiven and welcomed in Jesus Christ, and that the same Holy Spirit who raised Jesus from the dead is alive in us today. Our self-doubts will never be resolved by focusing more on ourselves; they will only be resolved by looking to Jesus—his presence, his power, his mercy, and his grace.

2   Barnabas Piper, *Help My Unbelief: Why Doubt Is Not the Enemy of Faith* (Charlotte: Good Book, 2020), 33, emphasis original.

Walking with God Anyway

If we think that Moses accepted God's answers to his objections, then we need to think again, because this was the point when Moses flatly told God to send someone else.

What God had promised him should have been enough. Wherever Moses went, God would go with him to empower him. Whatever Moses needed, God would provide. If Moses doubted his speaking ability, God would be right there to tell him what to say. God has made similar promises to us in Jesus Christ, who said, "I am with you always, to the end of the age" (Matt. 28:20). The promise of the Lord's presence ought to be enough for us, and it should have been enough for Moses, too.

Doubts or no doubts, we have to admire what Moses did next. The Bible does not give any clear or specific indication that his questions about his calling were resolved. I am not sure they were—at least not right away. But Moses walked with God anyway. God told Moses that his brother Aaron could be his spokesman (Ex. 4:16). Then God handed Moses a miraculous staff (Ex. 4:17). The next thing we know, Moses is standing in Pharaoh's court and saying, "Let my people go" (Ex. 5:1).

In the end, Moses did answer God's call. He was honest about his doubts. He took them to God in prayer. He stayed around long enough to hear what God had to say. Finally, when the moment of decision came, Moses did what God called him to do despite his lingering doubts. God said, "Go!" and Moses went.

Some people have the idea that before they can follow God, they have to get all their questions answered. We rarely if ever see this in the Bible. What we see instead is God calling people to follow him right away—people who will grow in faith *after* they begin to walk with God. Consider Job, who had all kinds of questions for the Almighty, which God never really answered. Instead, God came right back at Job with his own list of questions, until Job stepped back and worshiped. Or consider the first disciples. When Jesus called them to follow him, he did not enter into contract negotiations with them. He simply said, "Follow me" (e.g., Mark 1:17), and they left everything behind, no questions asked. But they did not become totally sure about Jesus until several years later, after he rose from the dead.

People who insist on getting all their doubts settled first never do follow Jesus—or get their questions answered, for that matter. The path of discipleship proves to be the way out of doubt, as many faithful Christians have discovered. The courageous German theologian Dietrich Bonhoeffer rightly said, "Only the obedient believe, and those who believe are obedient."[3] Missiologist Lesslie Newbigin made a similar point with added nuance:

> The confidence proper to a Christian is not the confidence of one who claims possession of demonstrable and indubitable knowledge. It is the confidence of one who had heard and answered the call that comes from the God through whom and for whom all things were made: "Follow me."[4]

---

3 Dietrich Bonhoeffer, *The Cost of Discipleship*, quoted in Lesslie Newbigin, *Proper Confidence: Faith, Doubt, and Certainty in Christian Discipleship* (Grand Rapids, MI: Eerdmans, 1995), 14–15.

4 Newbigin, *Proper Confidence*, 105.

The Scottish novelist George MacDonald took the same basic insight and turned it into a valuable caution for people who hesitate to trust and obey God: "Doubt may be a poor encouragement to do anything, but it is a bad reason to do nothing."[5]

Instead of doing nothing, we ought to start acting on what we know, because even when we have our doubts, there comes a point when we must still decide what we will do.

A man went out for dinner with a friend who felt drawn to Jesus Christ but still had her doubts. She told him that after months of going to church she wanted to become a Christian, but she couldn't take that step of faith because she had too many questions that she still didn't know how to answer. The man told her honestly that he didn't think she ever would get the answers to all her questions—at least not in this lifetime. But he wondered whether she could believe in Jesus simply on the basis of what she did know. Praise God, that was the moment she decided she was ready to give her life to Jesus. "You mean, right here in the restaurant?" he said. "Sure," she said, "Why not?"

Why not, indeed? Any place is a good place and any time is the right time to surrender our lives to Jesus Christ, notwithstanding our unanswered questions and lingering doubts. Following him will turn out to be the best decision we ever made.

What Happens When We Answer

When Moses decided to answer God's missional call, he began a life journey that drew him closer to God. This is what happens when doubters decide to walk with God: they learn to trust him

---

5 George MacDonald, *Lilith: A Romance* (1895; repr., London: Chatto & Windus, 2022), 126.

more and more. Sometimes they take extraordinary steps of faith, as Moses did.

What God did through Moses is quite a story. The prophet bravely went to Pharaoh's court and repeatedly told him to let God's people go. By the power of God, Moses brought down plagues from heaven. He parted the Red Sea. He led the children of Israel safely through the wilderness. He went up the mountain and spoke with God. Moses became so intimate with the Almighty that eventually he asked God to show him his glory. The man who once hid his face at the burning bush dared to gaze upon his Maker, unafraid. He came back down the mountain radiant with divine glory. He proclaimed God's law and pronounced God's judgment. He delivered God's people.

Moses had a unique role in the story of salvation, but each of us has a divine calling. How will we answer? What will we do with our doubts, and how will we pray through our questions? If we step out in brave obedience, as Moses did, our faith will grow as we answer God's call. God will prove himself faithful, and we will fulfill our unique purpose in the world.

In doing so, we will follow in the footsteps of our Savior. Jesus had a call upon his life, too—a call that consummated in his crucifixion. God the Father summoned God the Son to lifelong obedience leading up to his final sacrificial surrender to his fatherly will for the salvation of the world. Jesus was faithful every step of the way. Now, by his Spirit, the gift of his redemption is proclaimed by the people who follow him—people who, despite their doubts, believe enough to answer his call and stay on his mission.

*When the servant of the man of God rose early in
the morning and went out, behold, an army with
horses and chariots was all around the city. And the
servant said, "Alas, my master! What shall we do?"*

2 KINGS 6:15

4

Doubting God's Supernatural Protection

Elisha's Servant at Dothan

ACCORDING TO SOME EXPERTS, a strong desire for personal safety is one of the defining characteristics of Generation Z.[1] This character trait is often attributed to the effect of growing up after the terrorist attacks on 9/11 and of being raised by parents who were deeply concerned with protecting their sons and daughters.

Some people are critical of having too strong a desire to stay safe and sound. "Safety-ism," they call it.[2] But is it wrong to want to be protected from the harms and dangers of a fallen and

---

1   For a positive Christian response to young people's need for security, see Ben Simpson, "Gen Z and the Need for Safety," Burlap, February 27, 2018, https://www.thinkburlap .com/blog/gen-z-and-the-need-for-safety.

2   See, for example, Matthew Lesh, "Is Safetyism Destroying a Generation?," Institute of Public Affairs, September 3, 2018, https://ipa.org.au/publications-ipa/is-safetyism -destroying-a-generation.

sometimes frightful world? Many threats are real, and so are the fearful emotions they produce. According to 2023 data from the Centers for Disease Control, more than half of America's female students experienced "persistent feelings of sadness or hopelessness" during the previous year.[3] Given everything that is going wrong in the world, are these survey results really very surprising? And can we blame anyone—man or woman, young or old—for feeling discouraged or depressed?

Consider the testimony of Gracie Turner—a film major at Asbury University who was deeply affected by the spiritual awakening she experienced on her campus in Wilmore, Kentucky, during the winter of 2023. For four years, Gracie had been keeping a deep, dark secret from her evangelical classmates: she had lost her faith. During her high school years, as she watched one of her relatives waste away from cancer, as she witnessed domestic violence, and as she saw her family fall apart, she gradually lost confidence in God's willingness and ability to protect her.

Many young people can relate to Gracie's description of the way she felt: "I just remember thinking, why is this happening? How could this happen? And my first thought, or first person to blame, was God. I would lie in bed sometimes and just pray to God, like, it would be really nice if I didn't wake up tomorrow."[4]

Although Gracie continued to attend worship services, she stopped trusting Jesus to fix anything. Her life only seemed to get harder, not better, and her anxiety brought her to a spiritual

---

3 CDC data cited in Olivia Reingold, "Why Students in Kentucky Have Been Praying for 250 Hours," Real Clear Education, February 21, 2023, https://www.realclear education.com/.

4 Gracie Turner, quoted in Reingold, "Students in Kentucky."

breaking point. Finally, one Sunday morning she woke up and blurted to her roommate, "What if, instead of doing homework, we went to the chapel today?"[5]

There—by the power of the Holy Spirit—Gracie Turner met the living Christ. She heard the acoustic guitar, listened to her classmates sing God's praise, and suddenly became aware of his loving, protecting presence. "I just slumped down," she said. "It was the first time in a long time where I could finally just rest because I felt like I was at peace, and I was protected. I felt like it was God telling me, this is what you've been missing."[6]

Surrounded by Enemies

When the dangers around us are all too real, it is easy for us to doubt that anyone can keep us safe. Yet the Father's loving care, the Son's redeeming peace, and the Spirit's supernatural protection are much closer than we could ever imagine. One place to learn this is from the remarkable experience of Elisha's servant at Dothan.

This true Bible story comes from a time of military conflict in the Middle East. The king of Syria repeatedly led raiding parties into the territory of Israel, but his plans for conquest were thwarted just as repeatedly. Somehow, every time he planned an attack, the Israelites knew about it well in advance. By the time the Syrians reached their strategic military destination, the Israelites were already gone.

There was a reason why Syria's plans were frustrated: God was protecting his people. Specifically, as we read in 2 Kings 6, God's prophet Elisha was in charge of Israelite intelligence.

5 Turner, quoted in Reingold, "Students in Kentucky."
6 Turner, quoted in Reingold, "Students in Kentucky."

The man of God sent word to the king of Israel, "Beware that you do not pass this place, for the Syrians are going down there." And the king of Israel sent to the place about which the man of God told him. Thus he used to warn him, so that he saved himself there more than once or twice. (vv. 9–10)

Elisha thus proved to be "Israel's best line of defense."[7] It was as if he had the enemy under constant clandestine surveillance. By the Spirit of God, the prophet had inside information on what the Syrians were planning to do even before they did it. It happened over and over: God spied on the Syrians and revealed their plans to his prophet; Elisha informed Israel's king about their anticipated troop movements; the Israelites took evasive action; and the Syrians were foiled again.

After a while, the king of Syria could tell that there was a security leak somewhere—he just didn't know where. Understandably, he was desperate to know who the traitor was. "Greatly troubled because of this thing," he called for his servants and asked, "Will you not show me who of us is for the king of Israel?" (v. 11). One of them was brave enough to say, "None, my lord, O king; but Elisha, the prophet who is in Israel, tells the king of Israel the words that you speak in your bedroom" (v. 12). Today we might say that God's prophet was privy to the king's pillow talk.

As soon as the king of Syria knew that Elisha was the real culprit, he decided to take him captive. This is puzzling, because if the prophet always knew what the king would do before he did it, then wouldn't he know that the Syrians were coming to

7   Paul R. House, *1, 2 Kings*, New American Commentary (Nashville: Broadman & Holman, 1995), 276.

get him? Nevertheless, humanly speaking, Elisha was in grave danger. Syria's spies told their king that Elisha was at a place called Dothan. As soon as he heard this, the king "sent there horses and chariots and a great army, and they came by night and surrounded the city" (vv. 13–14). So many soldiers, simply to capture a solitary prophet! This foreshadows what happened on the night that Jesus was betrayed. Our Savior's enemies came to seize him in the garden of Gethsemane and brought "a great crowd with swords and clubs" to arrest him (Matt. 26:47). They did this even though he was unarmed, and even though all the armies in the world could never conquer the mighty Son of God. So too in Elisha's day, God's enemies sought to conquer God's servants with the sword.

When morning dawned, Dothan was under siege—a small city on a small hill surrounded by open countryside. When he woke up and looked around, Elisha's servant was terrified, and understandably so: "When the servant of the man of God rose early in the morning and went out, behold, an army with horses and chariots was all around the city." In that awful moment, when death was at his doorstep and there seemed to be no escape, Elisha's servant cried: "Alas, my master! What shall we do?" (2 Kings 6:15).

Even if we have never been besieged by hostile forces, we can relate to the servant's sense of panic. Sometimes we feel surrounded. Sometimes, too, we doubt that God can keep us safe—safe from fear, safe from hardship, safe from pain, or safe from people who try to hurt us. We face spiritual dangers as well, such as the perilous temptations and anxious thoughts that Satan uses to trouble our weary souls. Andrew Peterson sings about this transparently in the opening lines of one of his praise songs:

After all these years
I would've thought that all my fears were laid to rest
But I still get scared.[8]

We also get frightened from living in a culture that seems increasingly hostile to Christian faith—where it doesn't always feel safe to own the name of Jesus, or state the truth about God's design for human sexuality, or speak out against social injustice, or claim that there is one and only one way of salvation. The dangers are even greater in places where churches get attacked, where Christians are put under surveillance, and pastors get tossed in prison, such as China, Sudan, Turkey, India, or North Korea. In some dark places, the spiritual danger is palpable. In his book *City of God, City of Satan*, missiologist Robert Linthicum writes about the spiritual oppression he experienced in the city of Calcutta:

[A] spirit . . . , like a malevolent power, possessed and hovered over her city. The urban world's worst poverty, the indignity in which street people were forced to live, and the way the rich and the city's systems and structures disregarded it all now made sense—for a profoundly evil presence brooded over this city and held it in her thrall.[9]

What the Bible says is true, and we know it from our own experience: we "do not wrestle against flesh and blood, but against

8   "After All These Years," by Chad Cates, Andrew Peterson, and Randall Goodgame, track 1 on *After All These Years: A Collection*, produced by Harold Rubens and Andrew Peterson, Centricity Music, 2014.
9   Robert Linthicum, *City of God, City of Satan: A Biblical Theology of the Urban Church* (Grand Rapids, MI: Zondervan, 1991), 65.

the rulers, against the authorities, against the cosmic powers over this present darkness, against the spiritual forces of evil in the heavenly places" (Eph. 6:12). As we wrestle, sometimes we wonder, *Who will keep us safe from all these dangers?* We also ask what will happen to the people we love. In our anxiety, sometimes we sound like Elisha's servant: "Alas, my God; what shall we do?"

Protected by God

For his part, Elisha was totally and completely unafraid. This was not because he was unaware that he was in danger. Remember, the prophet always knew what Syria's armies were up to, so presumably he knew that they were coming to get him. Whether he knew about it in advance or not, early that morning Elisha too could see that he was surrounded. But despite the danger, God's faithful prophet remembered the most frequent exhortation in Holy Scripture and confidently repeated it to his servant: "Do not be afraid" (2 Kings 6:16). This is God's reassuring message to his people in every desperate circumstance and every dangerous situation: Do not fear! There is nothing for us to be afraid of.

What gave Elisha his serene sense of security? What enabled him to see the danger and stay unafraid? Simply this: he knew as a believer that he was safely protected by countless angels—the invincible army of the living God. So it was that the prophet told his servant not to be afraid, because "those who are with us are more than those who are with them" (2 Kings 6:16). His servant still couldn't see it. He thought they were outnumbered a thousand to two, but in fact they were more securely protected than he could possibly imagine.

The Bible frequently testifies to the authenticity of angels—God's innumerable, invincible army. For example, when Jacob went to meet Esau—with great trepidation, it must be said, because he had once betrayed his brother, who later became a powerful warrior—Scripture says that "the angels of God met him." And when he saw them, Jacob used a military term to describe their presence and exclaimed, "This is God's camp!" (Gen. 32:1–2). When King David—who knew a thing or two about mustering troops—tried to count the heavenly host, he found it impossible because

> the chariots of God are twice ten thousand,
>   thousands upon thousands. (Ps. 68:17)

David also knew that this mighty host stands ready to protect every believer:

> The angel of the LORD encamps
>   around those who fear him, and delivers them. (Ps. 34:7)

Or again:

> He will command his angels concerning you
>   to guard you in all your ways.
> On their hands they will bear you up. (Ps. 91:11–12)

One of the special ways God keeps his people safe is by sending guardian angels to protect us. What Elisha saw at Dothan was not unusual, therefore. It was unusual for him to see it, of course, because few mortals ever gaze on the army of God in all its fiery splendor. But that army is always there. Those who are for us really are greater than those who are against us, because God has countless angels at his disposal. As the epic poet John Milton said in his most famous sonnet, "Thousands at his bidding speed."[10] These numerous divine messengers are gentle enough to give us God's tender care, but also fierce enough to defend us against the deadliest foe. Even when we cannot see them, angels are *real*. One commentator writes:

> There is . . . [a] realm of reality—more actual, more factual, more substantial than anything we can see, hear, touch, taste, smell in this world. It exists all around us—not out there some-where, but *here*. There are legions of angels at our disposal, for which earth's forces have no countermeasures. . . . God and his squadrons of angels are everywhere around us—an encircling fire. We cannot see them with our natural eyes, but whether we see them or not, they are there. The earth is crammed with them![11]

In fact, God's fiery messengers are only a prayer away. This is what Elisha's servant experienced at Dothan. All he could see was an army of enemies. But then Elisha prayed that God would change the servant's perception: "O Lord, please open his eyes that he may see." And God promptly answered the prophet's

---

10 John Milton, "Sonnet on His Blindness," in *The Poetical Works of John Milton*, ed. Helen Darbishire (London: Oxford University Press, 1958), 437.

11 David Roper, *A Beacon in the Darkness*, ed. Larry R. Libby (Portland: Multnomah, 1995), 204, emphasis original.

prayer, as he loves to do: "So the Lord opened the eyes of the young man, and he saw, and behold, the mountain was full of horses and chariots of fire all around Elisha" (2 Kings 6:17). There was more for him to see than first met the eye. Elisha's servant thought he was surrounded by enemies, when in fact he was encompassed by the mighty angels of God, dressed for battle, standing guard over God's anointed servant.

What opened the servant's eyes and enabled him to see God's bright messengers was prayer. His experience teaches us that it is through intercession, primarily, that we perceive unseen spiritual realities. The angels were there all along, but to see them the way that Elisha could, the servant needed God the Holy Spirit to open his eyes. This was an answer to prayer. If we want to see God's work in the world, then we would do well to pray the prayer of Elisha: O Lord, open our eyes! Open our eyes to witness the work of your guardian angels. Open our eyes to see that you are there. Open our eyes to see that you are for us, not against us. Open our eyes to see that you have everything under control. Open our eyes to see that you are with us to protect us.

Fearless for Jesus

Knowing God's supernatural protection makes a powerful difference in the way we live. To begin with, it gives us more confidence to live and to die for Jesus. This is beautifully expressed in the answer to the first question in the Heidelberg Catechism—something every Christian should memorize. The question goes like this: "What is your only comfort in life and in death?" Then comes the life-shaping reply:

That I am not my own, but belong—body and soul, in life and in death—to my faithful Savior, Jesus Christ.

He has fully paid for all my sins with his precious blood, and has delivered me from the tyranny of the devil. He also watches over me in such a way that not a hair can fall from my head without the will of my Father in heaven; in fact, all things must work together for my salvation.

Because I belong to him, Christ, by his Holy Spirit, also assures me of eternal life and makes me wholeheartedly willing and ready from now on to live for him.[12]

Trusting in God's supernatural protection also empowers us to love our enemies, as Elisha did. That day at Dothan, God delivered the army of Syria directly into the prophet's hand. Ironically, at the same time God was opening the servant's eyes, he was also blinding the Syrians. But rather than destroying them, as he could have done, the prophet led them away peaceably, prepared them a lavish banquet, and then sent them safely back home to Syria (2 Kings 6:18–23). In doing this, Elisha was fulfilling a biblical imperative:

If your enemy is hungry, give him bread to eat,
and if he is thirsty, give him water to drink. (Prov. 25:21;
cf. Rom. 12:20)

The prophet was also giving us a picture of the gospel. "While we were [God's] enemies," the Bible says, God reconciled us to himself

---

12 *Creeds, Confessions, and Catechisms: A Reader's Edition*, ed. Chad Van Dixhoorn (Wheaton, IL: Crossway, 2022), 291.

"by the death of his Son" (Rom. 5:10). Then Jesus sat down with us at the love feast of the Lord's Supper to show that we are no longer God's enemies, but his friends.

Our Savior's loving welcome should make us equally fearless to love our enemies in Jesus's name. Too often, the world beyond the church feels our anger and senses our scorn. It is not hard for non-Christians to sense the contempt in our self-righteousness. Much too rarely they experience our love and mercy. But when we know how secure we are in Jesus, we can take the risk of sharing his hospitality, including with the people who reject us because they are in rebellion against God. The Holy Spirit wants to do more than keep us safe from our enemies; he wants us to win them through love.

Finally, trusting in God's eternal, supernatural protection empowers us to go into the world and preach the gospel, no matter what the cost. There is hardly a better example than the brave missionaries who went deep into the jungles of Ecuador in 1955 to reach the indigenous people we know today as the Huaorani. Jim and Elisabeth Elliot, Nate and Marjorie Saint, Ed and Marilou McCully, Pete and Olive Fleming, Roger and Barbara Youderian—their names are precious to God and his people. Operation Auca—as they called it—ended on January 8, 1956, when all five men were speared to death on the banks of the Curaray River.

But the story didn't end there. Several of the women bravely went back to the tribe, loving their enemies and leading many of them to faith in Christ. Forty years later, Nate Saint's son Steve decided to return to Ecuador and visit the men who murdered his father—enemies who had become friends through the gospel.

These men told him something remarkable. After the missionaries were slain, they said, some members of their tribe saw and heard a multitude of strange figures above the treetops. These *cowodi*—as they called them, using their word for strangers—were moving around, singing, and shining with light, brighter than any firefly in the jungle, with unblinking splendor. The Huaorani could tell that they were in the presence of something supernatural. The *cowodi* were a sign to them of a spiritual reality that was not fearful, like their own tribal deities, but peaceable and beautiful. Later, when they learned the Scriptures and came to saving faith in Jesus Christ, the Huaorani realized that they had been in the presence of guardian angels—angels who carried the men they martyred to glory.[13]

Whether we know it or not, God is watching over us from the cradle to the grave, and then on to glory. He has kept us safe more times than even we know. Whether we see them or not, his guardian angels are part of his protective care. Do not doubt, but believe that cherubim and seraphim are all around us, guarding us from danger as they proclaim God's holy praise. When we believe in God's supernatural protection, we too will be ready to live and to die for Jesus, to love our mortal enemies, and to bear any cost to carry the gospel to people who have never heard.

God has promised to protect us, deliver us, and guard us all our days. When we believe this, we are able to give the same testimony that King David gave—a testimony that Elisha and his servant could also have given, if only they had known the lyrics:

13 This story is recounted by Robert Jeffress, "Angels Minister to Us," Pathway to Victory, May 3, 2019, https://ptv.org/. See also Steve Saint, "Did They Have to Die?," *Christianity Today*, September 16, 1996, https://www.christianitytoday.com/.

Though an army encamp against me,
    my heart shall not fear;
though war arise against me,
    yet I will be confident. . . .

For he will hide me in his shelter
    in the day of trouble;
he will conceal me under the cover of his tent;
    he will lift me high upon a rock. (Ps. 27:3, 5)

Do not call me Naomi; call me Mara, for the Almighty has dealt very bitterly with me. I went away full, and the LORD has brought me back empty. Why call me Naomi, when the LORD has testified against me and the Almighty has brought calamity upon me?

RUTH 1:20–21

5

Doubting God's Abundant Generosity

Naomi on the Road to Bethlehem

IF GOD IS THERE, DOES HE EVEN CARE? Is he really as generous as people say he is? Sometimes, we have our doubts.

Voltaire certainly had his doubts. After a great earthquake struck the city of Lisbon in 1755, killing tens of thousands, the French Enlightenment philosopher mocked the theologians who tried to claim that somehow this natural disaster was under the sovereign hand of a benevolent God. In his famous "Poem on the Lisbon Disaster," Voltaire wrote:

> Come, ye philosophers, who cry, "All's well,"
> And contemplate this ruin of a world. . . .
> To those expiring murmurs of distress,
> To that appalling spectacle of woe,

Will ye reply: "You do but illustrate
The iron laws that chain the will of God"?[1]

In the aftermath of such a disaster, the philosopher claimed, no one would dare to suggest that God is working all things for good. Voltaire's opposition to Christianity and to Christ hardened over the years, until finally he came to believe "that instead of being a merciful, ameliorating, and benignant visitation, the religion of Christians would rather seem to be a scourge sent on man by the author of all evil."[2]

It is not just skeptics and atheists who doubt the goodness of God, however. Christians have their doubts too. C. S. Lewis famously wrestled with divine benevolence in *The Problem of Pain*—the book in which he tried to justify the ways of God to man. Before replying to the argument against God's generosity, Lewis framed the argument in the form of a logical syllogism: "If God were good, He would make His creatures perfectly happy, and if He were almighty He would be able to do what He wished. But the creatures are not happy. Therefore God lacks either goodness, or power, or both."[3]

Sooner or later, every one of us will wrestle with the reality of evil and the problem of pain. Sometimes doubts arise because

---

1   Voltaire, "Poem on the Lisbon Disaster" (1756), trans. Joseph McCabe, University of Washington, http://courses.washington.edu/hsteu302/Voltaire%20Lisbon%20Earthquake.html, accessed September 23, 2023.

2   Voltaire, quoted in "Gibbon; or, the Infidel Historian and His Protestant Editors," *The Dublin Review* 8 (February 1840): 208, https://www.google.com/books/edition/The_Dublin_Review/FOQLAQAAIAAJ?hl.

3   C. S. Lewis, *The Problem of Pain* (1940; repr., San Francisco: HarperCollins, 2002), 16.

of the evils we witness in the wider world and our sympathy for those who suffer. Where is God when floods rise and buildings crumble, when bombs fall and refugees flee for their lives, when disease and death spread across the globe? After the 2004 tsunami in the Indian Ocean that claimed more than two hundred thousand lives, one Asian newspaper echoed Lewis's argument when it pronounced: "If God is God, he's not good. If God is good, he's not God. You can't have it both ways, especially after the Indian Ocean catastrophe."[4]

Just as often, doubts arise because of our own personal misfortunes. We are tempted to think, *If God were good—good to me—then this wouldn't be happening.* Our trust in God's generosity tends to be circumstantial. When things are going well for us, it is easy to believe that he is good. But when things aren't going so well for us—as is so often the case—we have our doubts.

Why Naomi Was Bitter

Meet Naomi, on the road to Bethlehem. The old woman was deeply unhappy, and when we learn what happened to her, we understand why.

Naomi had known more than a few hardships. In time of famine, she and her husband, Elimelech, had left their native Israel and sought refuge in Moab, which was foreign soil. There they were able to find enough food, but Elimelech died not long afterward, leaving Naomi bereft of her husband. Still, she was able to make a life for herself. Her two sons married foreign brides, and for a decade things went reasonably well for the close-knit family.

---

4 Timothy Keller, *The Reason for God: Belief in an Age of Skepticism* (New York: Dutton, 2008), 23.

Then calamity struck again. We don't know why, but *both* of Naomi's sons died. The death of a child is the most painful loss any parent can ever suffer, but in the ancient world such a loss was much more than personal. A woman without the protection of male family members was particularly vulnerable. This is one of the reasons why the Bible places a special priority on the care of widows. If God doesn't help them—through his people—then who will?

As Naomi grieved her sad losses, she decided to end her sojourn and return to her native Bethlehem. The famine there was over, she had learned, and she longed to rejoin her people. Somewhat surprisingly, Naomi's two daughters-in-law decided to go with her—Ruth and Orpah. They were Moabites, not Israelites, so Naomi told them to stay behind: "Go, return each of you to her mother's house. May the LORD deal kindly with you, as you have dealt with the dead and with me. The LORD grant that you may find rest, each of you in the house of her husband!" (Ruth 1:8–9). Clearly, Naomi continued to believe in the God who is there. She pronounced a benediction over her beloved daughters-in-law, asking God to bless them with love and peace.

But, as their conversation continued, it became evident that it was not well with Naomi's soul. Ruth and Orpah put up a protest. Rather than going back home to Moab, they wanted to journey to Bethlehem with Naomi. She responded with these bitter words:

> Turn back, my daughters; why will you go with me? Have I yet sons in my womb that they may become your husbands? Turn back, my daughters; go your way, for I am too old to have a husband. If I should say I have hope, even if I should have a husband

this night and should bear sons, would you therefore wait till they were grown? Would you therefore refrain from marrying? No, my daughters, for it is exceedingly bitter to me for your sake that the hand of the LORD has gone out against me. (Ruth 1:11–13)

Naomi had nothing left to give to Ruth and Orpah. She could not provide them a happy home or offer them husbands to start new families. But her real complaint was that Almighty God was against her. She knew that he was there, and in fact that was the problem! What Naomi disputed was God's personal generosity— his goodness to *her*. She did not doubt his existence but doubted his character. He may be there, but does he even care? Naomi was skeptical, as we sometimes are.

Naomi's denial of divine beneficence becomes even clearer at the end of the chapter, when she finally gets back to Bethlehem and her old friends can hardly recognize her. "Is this Naomi?" they asked (Ruth 1:19). Because of how much she had aged, and how disfigured she was by her distress, they couldn't believe it was really Naomi. In response, the old woman disavowed her very name. "Naomi" means "pleasant," which under the circumstances seemed too painfully ironic. Better to call her "bitter," which in Hebrew is the word *mara*. So here is the name change she demanded from the folks in her hometown:

Do not call me Naomi [Pleasant]; call me Mara [Bitter], for the Almighty has dealt very bitterly with me. I went away full, and the LORD has brought me back empty. Why call me Naomi [Pleasant], when the LORD has testified against me and the Almighty has brought calamity upon me? (Ruth 1:20–21)

It was quite a speech. The Bible does not tell us how the good people of Bethlehem responded, but we can imagine that Naomi's words were greeted with stunned silence. Has anyone ever launched a more direct assault on God's generosity? Naomi accused the Almighty of taking away what she had, of acting against her, of making her life miserable. Is God really for us? Does he truly have our best interests at heart? Will he indeed make all things work together for our good? Naomi had her doubts! In fact, as far as she could tell, God was responsible for all her misfortune.

We can hardly blame Naomi for feeling this way. In fact, we may secretly sympathize. We too have had our doubts. We lost a loved one. We went through hard times financially. We got our hopes up and then they were dashed. We didn't get what we wanted and maybe needed and probably thought we deserved. We continued to struggle with chronic illness. We never lived the dream, only the nightmare, and then the conclusion seemed obvious: God is not good. Take the old Sunday school song, change a single word, and it may feel like a better fit for our bitter circumstances:

> God is not good,
> God is not good,
> God is not good,
> he's not good to me.

How God Cared for Naomi

As long as Naomi was singing that bitter tune, it is doubtful whether she was very good company. People who complain about everything have a way of sucking the joy out of life—not just for themselves, but for everyone around them.

68

Naomi's embittered spirit makes Ruth's commitment all the more remarkable. When her mother-in-law told her to stay home with her own people, Ruth made one of the most astonishing vows in the Bible. With her bitter complaints, Naomi was just about the last person anyone would want to be around. But Ruth said: "Do not urge me to leave you or return from following you. For where you go I will go, and where you lodge I will lodge. Your people shall be my people, and your God my God. Where you die I will die, and there will I be buried" (Ruth 1:16–17). With these bold promises, Ruth made her life-and-death commitment to the true and living God, and also to her mother-in-law.

Ruth's promise was a life-giving blessing to Naomi. Doubters do not necessarily need someone to answer all their questions. They probably do not want a lot of unsolicited advice, even good advice. But doubters do need believers who refuse to give up on them. They need someone to stay with them when their faith is sinking down—someone who shows them a loving example of trusting in the living God, as Ruth did when she walked alongside Naomi all the way back to Bethlehem.

When our faith is strong, we should not turn away from friends who are struggling spiritually but stay with them on their journey and then see what God will do. Keith Johnson contends that showing mercy

> means walking alongside someone with doubt as they work through their questions and problems. Christians sometimes pull away from doubters because the presence of doubt poses a challenge and brings discomfort. But a person dealing with

doubt should never have to walk alone. Christians should seek out and embrace those who doubt with the goal not of fixing them but of loving and encouraging them.[5]

When we walk beside one another in seasons of struggle, something amazing happens: we experience God's loving goodness. Ruth's commitment showed Naomi something more than the love of Ruth; it also showed her the love of God. Naomi was grieving, Naomi was empty. Naomi felt that God was against her. Yet at the very moment she was making these cynical complaints, God was already at work—including through her daughter-in-law—to show her his abundant grace. She just couldn't see it yet!

At the very moment when Naomi was pulling away, God was reaching out to pull her in and bring her close, as he often does. No one has more patience with people who have their doubts than God does. He loves to put his own words into practice: "Have mercy on those who doubt" (Jude 22). We often see this in the Psalms, where the singers of Israel reveal their secret doubts. "Why do you hide yourself in times of trouble?" they ask (Ps. 10:1), "How long, O Lord? Will you forget me forever?" (Ps. 13:1). "Have you not rejected us, O God?" (Ps. 108:11). Yet the psalmists also see God beginning to work, and in those very songs they express their hope in God's goodness:

> O Lord, you hear the desire of the afflicted;
> you will strengthen their heart. (Ps. 10:17)

---

5 Keith Johnson, "Doubt," in *Life Questions Every Student Asks: Faithful Responses to Common Issues*, ed. Gary M. Burge and David Lauber (Downers Grove, IL: InterVarsity Press, 2020), 141.

I will sing to the LORD,

> because he has dealt bountifully with me. (Ps. 13:6)

There are many signs of God's generosity in Naomi's story—and we can see signs of God's mercy in our own stories, too, if only we learn to pay close attention. Naomi had suffered the loss of loved ones, but Ruth was still by her side. God did not leave her without a family; he gave her a daughter-in-law who stayed closer than a sister. Naomi said she was empty. Yet in the providence of God she arrived in Bethlehem—note carefully—"at the beginning of the barley harvest" (Ruth 1:22). The Bible never wastes a detail, and the coming of harvest time sets the stage for everything that follows. Naomi may have felt empty, but she was coming to a place of abundance, where God had made the fields ripe with grain. However empty she may have felt, God's plan was in motion, and therefore she was moving in the direction of fullness.

By the time we get to the end of the story, Ruth will have met her new husband Boaz, Naomi will have found a redeemer to restore her family lands, and their household will have received the precious gift of a baby boy, who would turn out to be the grandfather of King David. Naomi may have started this journey empty, but by the time God had worked his plan, he had filled her lap with a grandson to love and cherish (see Ruth 4:16). Then she knew that God had been good—so good!—to her.

God has generous plans for us as well, even if our present disappointment causes us to doubt. Usually, we recognize God's good purpose better in retrospect. We see it better backward, but by faith we can also choose to believe it forward! Naomi did not have to wait until God gave her a grandson. She could have believed that God was good on the road to Bethlehem. We do not have to wait, either. Even before we see what God is up to, we can believe his plan for our redemption, especially if we remember well what he has done for us in the past. When the Bible says that "all things work together for good" (Rom. 8:28), we can trust this when we are on our knees, not just when we are looking in the rearview mirror. We should know God well enough by now to know as well that we can count on him to come through.

The ultimate proof of this principle—believing forward—is the cross of Christ. At the time that Jesus was crucified, it must have seemed that evil had triumphed, that all God's purposes had failed. But the death of Jesus was the death of death, the undoing of the devil, and the end of all our sin. Even as the soldiers led him toward Calvary, God was setting in motion the plan that would lead to the salvation of the world. Not even this ultimate evil—the murder of God's one and only Son—was outside God's power to work all things for good. Jesus believed this already on the road to Calvary, three days before he rose from the grave. "For the joy that was set before him," Jesus "endured the cross, despising the shame" (Heb. 12:2). He did this trusting all the while in the resurrection power of God the Holy Spirit.

We need to take whatever doubts we have about the goodness of God to Calvary, where God in Christ suffered the greatest miseries of human pain. Tim Keller describes what happens when we ask the question "Why does God allow evil and suffering to continue?" from the vantage point of the cross. "We still do not know what the answer is," Keller says. "However, we now know what the answer isn't. It can't be that he doesn't love us. It can't be that he is indifferent or detached from our condition. God takes our misery and suffering so seriously that he was willing to take it on himself."[6] George MacDonald drew a similar connection between our Savior's suffering and our own. "The Son of God," he preached, "suffered unto the death, not that men might not suffer, but that their suffering might be like his, and lead them up to his perfection."[7] When we believe in what Jesus did for us on the cross, we can also believe this with absolute certainty: he will work what seems to be bad in our lives for good, too, just as he did when Jesus not only died but also rose again.

How God Changed Naomi

There is something else God did for Naomi. Certainly, she saw a change in her circumstances, which is what we usually hope and pray will happen when we are disappointed with God. We want God to take away whatever is hard for us and give us what we desire. But God usually has a more important change he wants to bring: a change inside us. And more often than not, he changes us *before* he changes our circumstances (if he ever does, which he doesn't always).

Naomi is a perfect example. As her story unfolds, we see her acting in faith, even when she still has her doubts—a clear sign that God is turning her cynical doubt to sweet belief. Naomi trusted God enough to go back home to Bethlehem, and back to the people of God. Too often, when people have their doubts, the first thing they do is stop going to church. What we ought to do is exactly the opposite: go back to worship with the people of

6 Keller, *The Reason for God*, 30–31.

7 George MacDonald, *Unspoken Sermons: Series I, II, III in One Volume* (n.p.: NuVision, 2007), 21.

God, as Naomi did. There we will find people who can empathize with our doubts and will walk with us as we work through them, as Naomi also did.

Shortly after the two women arrived in Bethlehem, Ruth found a field where she could gather some grain. Naomi saw this for what it was: a sign of God's generous grace. In response, she pronounced a benediction on Boaz, the man who owned the field. "Blessed be the man who took notice of you," she said to Ruth. "May he be blessed by the LORD, whose kindness has not forsaken the living or the dead!" (Ruth 2:19–20). Through her struggle with doubt, Naomi could see that in his loving-kindness, God was beginning to work. Her heart was starting to soften. She believed in his goodness at least enough to pray for his blessing in the lives of her loved ones.

God has a change he wants to work in us as well, especially when we have trouble believing in his abundant generosity. He wants our faith to grow. One way for us to experience this change is simply to start noticing all the ways that God *has* been good to us. Gratitude is good soil for growing our faith. Rather than focusing on the things he hasn't done, start listing the things he has done. The well-known words of an old hymn may seem trite, but they also happen to be helpful:

Count your blessings,
name them one by one;
Count your many blessings,
see what God hath done.[8]

---

8   Johnson Oatman, "Count Your Blessings" (1897), https://hymnary.org/.

When Naomi started to count her blessings, she discovered how many reasons she had to give God praise: a safe return home, a family member who cared for her, more than enough food to eat, and the hope of a redeemer. Naomi's blessings give us a head start on our own lists: a place to live, food to eat, people who love us, and most of all the redemption we have in Jesus—forgiveness through his blood, with the certain hope of eternal life, by the power of the empty tomb. As we count our blessings—literally enumerating the things that God has done for us—we get a better, truer perspective on life. We stop focusing exclusively on our problems and start thinking about how to bless other people, as Naomi did.

There is something else we can do when we are struggling to see that God is good, and that is to persist in prayer. Even when we are doubtful, we can still ask God to help us, praying with as much faith as we can muster.

The apostle James assures us that whenever we need anything, we should ask for it, because God "gives generously to all without reproach" (James 1:5). James also says that we should "ask in faith, with no doubting" (James 1:6). His point is not that having our doubts somehow cancels the efficacy of our prayers. His point rather is that we should not let our doubts get in the way of persisting in prayer. Keith Johnson clarifies the apostle's meaning in ways that underscore God's goodness:

> James's primary purpose in this passage is to point to God's generosity. He is saying that because God does not hold back from helping his people, no one should hold themselves back from God. A person in need should ask God for help with

confidence that they will receive this help. A doubter in this instance is someone who does not ask God for help because they assume God will not give it.[9]

We should never hold back from asking God for what we truly need. He is a generous giver. The more we ask, and then wait patiently for God to answer, the more we will see how good he is.

How God Helps Our Unbelief

Naomi had to wait for God to work, but the ultimate proof of his goodness came on the day she became a grandmother—when Ruth put a grandson on her lap, a child the townspeople called "a restorer of life" (Ruth 4:15).

Ruth's baby was the proof that God had heard Naomi's prayer for blessing. In fact, God answered her prayer more generously than she could possibly have imagined. God's blessing on Boaz turned out to be a blessing for us as well—the blessing of a grandson. But that blessing was only the beginning. The answer to prayer that spilled over into Naomi's life spills over into our lives too: her grandson turned out to be the grandfather of King David, whose greatest descendant proved to be the Savior of the world.

The gift of a grandson also showed Naomi that there was life after death. The book of Ruth began with three funerals, but it ended with a baby shower. This is the kind of grace we get only from a God who holds the power of eternal life. In *The Reason for God*, Tim Keller argues:

9   Johnson, "Doubt," 135.

The Biblical view of things is resurrection—not a future that is just a *consolation* for the life we never had but a *restoration* of the life you always wanted. This means that every horrible thing that ever happened will not only be undone and repaired but will in some way make the eventual glory and joy even greater.[10]

What Naomi experienced is like the scene in *The Lord of the Rings* when humble Sam meets the great wizard Gandalf after his deadly descent into the abyss. "I thought you were dead!" Sam exclaims. "But then I thought I was dead myself!" This makes the hobbit wonder: "Is everything sad going to come untrue?"[11]

We want to believe that the answer is yes, not just in the face of death but through all the struggles we have in this fallen world. We want to believe that everything sad will come untrue, that in his goodness God is powerful enough to make things right again.

In an article entitled "When Bleeding Hearts Break," medical missionary Eric McLaughlin writes honestly about the empty despair he sometimes feels, and also about his sudden discovery of God's abundant generosity. His spiritual breakthrough came on a day when he was busy answering questions over email regarding his work in Burundi, where he encounters long lines of suffering patients every day. A supporter back home wrote to ask, "How have you overcome the fear of hoping in order to reach for God's promise of hope?"

It was a good and fair question—sober about life's suffering while at the same time expectant about God's work in the world.

10 Keller, *The Reason for God*, 32, emphases original.
11 J. R. R. Tolkien, *The Return of the King*, part 3 of *The Lord of the Rings* (New York: Houghton Mifflin, 1993), 930.

Still, the missionary doctor was undone. "As soon as I read the question, my heart sank, because the question was asking how I did something that I felt utterly incapable of doing."

Some of McLaughlin's patients made it hard for him to hope. He thought instantly of Odette, a young woman in her twenties who was hospitalized with kidney failure. She suffered so terribly that most people wondered how she found the will to live. Odette's family scraped together enough money to send her to a specialist, but McLaughlin doubted it would make a difference. Since long-term dialysis was not an option, why bother to see a specialist?

As McLaughlin sat at his computer, unable to affirm that he had any way to overcome "the fear of hoping," his phone chimed insistently with a series of text messages. The messages came from a former student who worked at a hospital in a nearby city, who wrote:

Good morning doctor. / I just wanted to let you know that we have been caring for Odette. / The young woman that you had seen last month. / We have not been able to do much. / But some fluids and careful observation have resulted in her kidneys returning almost to normal! / We're sending her home today. / I just thought you would want to know. / Praise God!

As he read this series of messages, McLaughlin found his hope rising in the goodness of God, to the point of praise. Here is how he described what his student's message meant to him:

This was all fantastic and encouraging, but what really struck me was that the message arrived precisely when I was sitting there thinking about how afraid I was to hope and how I had no idea how to reply to those asking me how to hope. I turned my head and saw my own reflection in the glass of the window-pane. The idea that God was present was no longer theoretical; it was real and sudden. In a moment, the revealing of this whole story filled me with tearful joy, not a small amount of fear, and a renewed hope.[12]

As we wait for our own next glimpse of God's abundant generosity, we should not be afraid to hope. We should not stop counting our blessings or asking for what we truly need. God is working his plan. In fact, he has already set it in motion. Soon we will see again how good he is—so good!—to us.

---

12 Eric McLaughlin, "When Bleeding Hearts Break," *Christianity Today*, July/August 2022, 56.

But as for me, my feet had almost stumbled,
    my steps had nearly slipped.
For I was envious of the arrogant
    when I saw the prosperity of the wicked.

PSALM 73:2–3

6

Doubting God's Basic Fairness

Asaph outside God's Temple

IMAGINE A CLIMBER CLINGING to a sheer rock face, thousands of feet above the ground. The mountaineer is on a free solo, without any protective equipment: no ropes, no cleats or crampons, no safety harness. One false move means certain death.

Now imagine the solitary climber feeling a foothold give way or scrabbling for a handhold and missing. Imagine the sudden fear of falling, and then the relief of holding on and still having a chance to make it to the top.

This was Asaph's experience with faith and doubt. The psalmist had been making good progress on the "free solo" of life. Like a climber near the summit, he was clinging faithfully to the God of Israel, when suddenly he felt the rock face start to give way. Later, when he put this experience into writing, he said, "As for me, my feet had almost stumbled" (Ps. 73:2).

In that desperate moment, Asaph nearly gave up the faith, let go of God, and fell to his spiritual death. It was a very close call. Anyone who has ever struggled with doubt knows how easy it is to lose your spiritual grip. But at the very last moment, something happened to Asaph that saved him. Thank God, a move Asaph made when he was in danger of falling strengthened his hold and rescued his soul. Hearing his testimony can help us get a grip too, especially when we have our doubts about God's fundamental fairness.

When Good Things Happen to Bad People

After King David, Asaph may be the Bible's most famous singer-songwriter. We know this man mainly through his lyrics. Think of him as a worship leader who became a recording artist. Psalm 73 is one of a dozen worship songs that the Psalter attributes to his authorship.

Asaph began the way we might expect a godly musician to begin a worship song, with a strong note of praise:

> Truly God is good to Israel,
>> to those who are pure in heart. (v. 1)

There is no hint of doubt in these opening lines. Asaph expresses the praise of a grateful nation and highlights the importance of personal faith. It takes a pure heart to see God, and this was the songwriter's own testimony. He believed in the goodness of God.

As the song continues, however, we discover that Asaph struggled with serious doubts about the very truth claim he made in verse 1. Verses 2 through 14 describe his crisis of faith. Is God indeed good to his people? There was a time when Asaph wasn't so sure. Yes, many people believe God is good. "But as for me," he wrote,

> my feet had almost stumbled,
>> my steps had nearly slipped. (v. 2)

Notice that Asaph was speaking of his past. Verse 1 is his present perspective—his faith-filled conclusion. But the verses that follow give us a flashback to the season of skeptical doubts that almost became the worship leader's spiritual downfall. In its rendering of verse 2, the New International Version describes his close call like this:

> My feet had almost slipped;
>> I had nearly lost my foothold.

In the rest of Psalm 73, Asaph tells us why he almost fell away from the faith and also what God did to strengthen his grip. What he couldn't understand was why good things happened to bad people. It made him extremely jealous. "For I was envious of the arrogant," he says in verse 3, "when I saw the prosperity of the wicked." It's just not fair! If God is good, then obviously he will do good to those who are good and punish wrongdoers. And yet, as Asaph looked at what was happening in the world, he saw exactly the opposite. The righteous were struggling. Meanwhile, evildoers were getting away with murder, sometimes literally.

With brutal honesty, here is how the singer-songwriter described the lifestyles of the rich and infamous:

For they have no pangs until death;
>> their bodies are fat and sleek.
They are not in trouble as others are;
>> they are not stricken like the rest of mankind.
Therefore pride is their necklace;
>> violence covers them as a garment.
Their eyes swell out through fatness;
>> their hearts overflow with follies.
They scoff and speak with malice;
>> loftily they threaten oppression.
They set their mouths against the heavens,
>> and their tongue struts through the earth. (vv. 4–9)

As far as Asaph could tell, the ungodly are free from earthly cares. They always get their way, often at the expense of other people. They are arrogant and violent—everything God hates. Nothing is sacred to these people. They mock the Almighty and still go unscathed.

In fact, the more evil they perform, the more popular the ungodly become. We witness the same phenomenon in today's celebrity culture, where so many things contrary to Scripture are regarded as morally superior: self-promotion, so-called sexual freedom, and the promotion of abortion and other ungodly practices. The popularity of unrighteousness leads many people astray. Rather than turning back to God, the people of Israel in Asaph's day turned toward wrongdoing (v. 10). They gave their "likes" and their "follows" to ungodliness. And they thought they could get away with it. "How can God know?" they scoffed. "Is there knowledge in the Most High?" (v. 11).

It's quite a list. We sense that by the time Asaph was finished, he was not only envious but also embittered.[1] Here is how he summarized what he witnessed:

Behold, these are the wicked;
　　always at ease, they increase in riches. (v. 12)

"Take a look," he basically was saying. "The ungodly are healthy, wealthy, and famous."

It all seemed so unfair. The righteous ought to be rewarded, while the wicked get punished. Yet for Asaph this wasn't really a justice issue. His concern was more selfish. Seeing the wicked prosper made him doubt whether it was worth all the sacrifices he made to serve the living God. He said:

All in vain have I kept my heart clean
　　and washed my hands in innocence.
For all the day long I have been stricken
　　and rebuked every morning. (vv. 13–14)

Walking with God was a struggle for Asaph, as it is for most believers. And when he saw how wealthy the ungodly were, and how trouble free their lives seemed to be, he doubted whether it was worth the daily effort to keep himself pure.

Today we might diagnose Asaph's condition as spiritual FOMO—"the fear of missing out." The singer-songwriter felt shortchanged. Here he was, investing his life in the service of

---

1　Michael F. Ross, *The Light of the Psalms: Deepening Your Faith with Every Psalm* (Fearn, Ross-Shire, UK: Christian Focus, 2006), 132.

God, but he didn't seem to be getting much out of it. His righteousness felt so undercompensated that he was ready to walk away from God. If the ungodly were happier anyway, then ministry seemed like a huge waste of time. There just wasn't enough in it for him.

If we haven't felt the temptation yet to live selfishly rather than generously, someday we will. It will appear easier to make money than to give it away. It will seem more enjoyable to sleep in on Sunday morning than to get up and serve people at church. It will feel better to give in to sexual sin than to protect someone else's purity. In one way or another, it will seem more beneficial to turn away from God than to follow him.

We may find Asaph's honesty refreshing. When Job, similarly, made his epic complaint against God, he celebrated his authenticity. One biblical paraphrase has Job telling God,

> I'm not keeping one bit of this quiet,
> > I'm laying it all out on the table;
> > my complaining to high heaven is bitter, but honest.
> > (Job 7:11 MSG)

Asaph also put all his cards on the table (so to speak), and his objections raise serious questions for us as well. What difference does it make to follow Christ, except to make our lives more miserable and less enjoyable? Sometimes we can sympathize with the man who considered the claims of Christianity and concluded that "God performed no observable function and had no valid purpose."[2]

---

2   S. A. Joyce, quoted in Timothy Keller, *Making Sense of God: An Invitation to the Skeptical* (New York: Viking, 2016), 29.

As we think about the possibilities and consider the alternatives, our feet start to slip.

Before exploring what changed Asaph's mind, notice that his premise is debatable. Is it really true that atheists and agnostics lead happier lives? In fact, ample research shows that life is *better* for people with Christian convictions. In an article entitled "No, Christianity Is Not as Bad as You Think," Josh Howerton documents that Christian communities experience less depression, less suicide, less addiction, and less abuse. At the same time, Christians give more generously, receive more social support, enjoy more satisfaction, and have more opportunities to do something meaningful with their lives. They even have better sex and happier children.[3]

If all that is true, then Asaph's premise was flawed in the first place. The unrighteous should be pitied, not envied. Yet sometimes we are tempted to see the world the way Asaph did and think that sinners have much more fun.

There is another flaw in Asaph's thinking that we should be sure to notice. When it came to fairness, Asaph was mainly or exclusively thinking about himself. But there are much more important justice concerns in the world that ought to be more important to us than getting what we think we deserve. What about widows and orphans? What about the survivors of warfare and persecution? What about the poor and the oppressed? If God

---

3 Josh Howerton, "No, Christianity Is Not as Bad as You Think," TGC, March 19, 2022, https://www.thegospelcoalition.org/. See also Philip Yancey, *A Skeptic's Guide to Faith: What It Takes to Make the Leap* (Grand Rapids, MI: Zondervan, 2009), 132, where Yancey summarizes Dr. David Larson's research and concludes that people "who attend church regularly, pray, and read their Bibles are hospitalized less often, recover from surgery faster, have stronger immune systems, and live longer."

is truly just, then he must have some plan to right these wrongs. But at the moment, Asaph was too preoccupied to show care or concern for the world's greater injustices.

Where Asaph Went

Something happened to Asaph that changed his perspective entirely. We first sense that his thinking shifted in Psalm 73:15:

> If I had said, "I will speak thus,"
>> I would have betrayed the generation of your children.

Suddenly, we realize that everything in Psalm 73:2–14 was hypothetical. These were all things that Asaph started to think but held back from saying until he had time to think things through.

There is an important caution for us here. Asaph realized that his doubts could have a negative spiritual influence on the people around him. If he denied the fairness of God, that would have been a betrayal of God, of course, but it also would have betrayed Asaph's faith community—the people he loved and served. The worship leader didn't want to drag them down with his skeptical doubts, so he kept some of his thoughts private while he was working things out with God.

We should be honest about our spiritual struggles, especially when we can process them with mature believers who have had their own doubts and can help us reason our way back to God. But we need to recognize that we are not the only people affected by our doubts. We should be careful not to discourage the people around us—especially newer, younger Christians—with negative spiritual thoughts we are still struggling to work through. We should never pretend, but we should doubt our doubts and fight our tendency to disbelieve.

When Asaph had his doubts, he didn't drag other people down with him. Instead, he did the one thing that could and did make the biggest difference in his relationship with God: worn out by his spiritual struggle, he went to worship anyway. Before he lost his spiritual grip—before he reached any wrong conclusions about the fairness of God—he went back to the temple. Here is how he described that faith-strengthening, doubt-challenging, foothold-stabilizing moment:

> But when I thought how to understand this,
>   it seemed to me a wearisome task,
> until I went into the sanctuary of God. (Ps. 73:16–17)

Asaph's personal experience of being in God's holy presence changed everything. At the temple he had such a massive paradigm shift that he wanted to take back all the bitter things he had been thinking about God and was tempted to say out loud. He worshiped God even when he didn't really feel like worshiping God (which, by the way, is something that happens to worship leaders too), and this strengthened his spiritual grip.

Something similar happened to the contemporary poet Christian Wiman, who writes about his experience in his widely read essay "Gazing into the Abyss." Wiman had been diagnosed with a rare and incurable form of blood cancer on his thirty-ninth birthday, of all days. At the time, he had been married for less than a year. Understandably, he and his wife were devastated. "Then one morning," he writes, we found ourselves going to church. *Found ourselves.* That's exactly what it felt like, in both senses of the phrase, as if some impulse in each of us had finally been catalyzed into action, so that we were casting aside the Sunday paper and moving toward the door with barely a word between us; and as if, once inside the church, we were discovering exactly where and who we were meant to be. That first service was excruciating, in that it seemed to tear all wounds wide open, and it was profoundly comforting, in that it seemed to offer the only possible balm.[4]

In one sense, there was nothing extraordinary about what either Asaph or the Wimans experienced. All they did was walk into an ordinary worship service. Yet what happened there was profound, because they entered into the presence of the true and living God and gained a perspective there to keep them from slipping and falling, or to offer the hope of consolation.

One way to understand the difference that worship makes is to follow the pronouns in Psalm 73.[5] The praise song begins with a God-centered focus: "Truly God is good." Yet in verse 2 Asaph decides to take what might be called a spiritual selfie: "But as for me." Is it really surprising that as soon as he turns the lens back on himself, he starts to struggle? Then, from verses 4 to 12, nearly all the pronouns are "they," "their," and "them." Rather than taking responsibility for his own spiritual situation, he compares himself

4   Christian Wiman, "Gazing into the Abyss," *The American Scholar*, June 1, 2007, https://theamericanscholar.org/, emphasis original.
5   James Montgomery Boice, *Psalms*, vol. 2, *Psalms 42–106* (Grand Rapids, MI: Baker, 1996), 615.

to others, which does not help him in his relationship with God at all. It is only when he turns from "me" and "they" to "you," the Lord, that he gains proper perspective.

This is not to say that somehow going to church automatically solves all our problems or resolves all our doubts. We bring our spiritual struggles with us into worship, and sometimes being with God and with people who believe in God sharpens our skepticism. Yet God has promised to be present by his Holy Spirit when we worship. Jesus promised that wherever two or three of us gather in his name, he is right there with us (Matt. 18:20). The Bible assures us that through the blood of Jesus we draw near to God and enter the Most Holy Place (Heb. 10:19–22). It says further that when we come to worship, we are not alone but join myriads of angels and the saints who have gone before us—as well as Jesus himself—at the throne of Almighty God (Heb. 12:22–24). There is no better place for us to have a fresh encounter with our Savior than the place where he has promised to meet us: in public worship that is grounded in the gospel.

When we truly worship, we acknowledge God for who he is. We stop speculating about God and start praising him.[6] We remember that he is God and we are not. We don't even think about our experience of God, for this too can get in the way of our spiritual recovery. We simply praise God himself. In his writings on faith and doubt, Herman Bavinck wisely concluded that "the locus of confidence is not in the competence of one's own knowing, but in the faithfulness and reliability of the one who is known. The

6 Derek Kidner, *Psalms 73–150*, Tyndale Old Testament Commentaries (Downers Grove, IL: InterVarsity Press, 2009), 261–62.

weight of confidence rests there and not here with us."[7] Worship shifts the focus off ourselves and provides a secure foothold for our faith in the triune God.

What Asaph Saw

When Asaph went to the temple and worshiped, he saw something new that in a split second turned his doubt to faith. What he saw was simply this: how the story ends. Before he arrived at God's temple, all he could see was how much healthier and wealthier he would be if he turned away from God. Then he stepped into God's sanctuary and there, the songwriter tells us, "I discerned their end" (Ps. 73:17). In other words, he suddenly realized that because of the justice of God, eventually the wicked would be condemned.

Asaph expands on this theme as Psalm 73 continues. What will happen to the ungodly?

> Truly you set them in slippery places;
>   you make them fall to ruin.
> How they are destroyed in a moment,
>   swept away utterly by terrors!
> Like a dream when one awakes,
>   O Lord, when you rouse yourself, you despise them as
>   phantoms. (vv. 18–20)

Asaph picks up on this idea again in verse 27, even more emphatically:

7   Lesslie Newbigin, *Proper Confidence: Faith, Doubt, and Certainty in Christian Disciple-ship* (Grand Rapids, MI: Eerdmans, 1995), 67.

For behold, those who are far from you shall perish;
    you put an end to everyone who is unfaithful to you.

Admittedly, thinking about the end of life and the hereafter makes some people more fearful. The great novelist Leo Tolstoy wrestled with his doubts about death in his *Confession*:

> My question—that which at the age of fifty brought me to the verge of suicide—was the simplest of questions, lying in the soul of every man . . . a question without an answer to which one cannot live. It was: "What will come of what I am doing today or tomorrow? What will come of my whole life? Why should I live, why wish for anything, or do anything?" It can also be expressed thus: Is there any meaning in my life that the inevitable death awaiting me does not destroy?[8]

Unless we know that in the end God will do what is merciful and just, thinking ahead to the end of our earthly existence may well lead us to despair. But Asaph had the opposite experience. For him, the end of the world was the beginning of hope.

Asaph knew that on the one hand the wicked would fall under the justice of God, the righteous Judge. Their apparent success was only a dream, not reality. *They* were the ones on a slippery slope, not Asaph! In a moment, their lives would be lost and everything they worked so hard to gain would fall from their grasp. Without any reason to hope in God, they would be terrified every time they thought about dying—a terror no one can escape. After that,

---

8 Leo Tolstoy, *A Confession*, quoted in Timothy Keller, *The Reason for God: Belief in an Age of Skepticism* (New York: Dutton, 2008), 201.

they would face final judgment, where the fairness of God would destroy their proud oppression.

At the same time, Asaph saw that in the end the righteous would receive their merciful reward. Now we know how this happens: by the surrender of the Son of God to the very injustice that harms us and angers us. Tim Keller writes:

> It is only in Jesus that we see how radically and literally God identified with the poor and oppressed. He was born to a poor family; he lived among the marginalized and outcast. His trial was a miscarriage of justice. He died violently, naked and penniless. And so the Son of God himself knew what it was like to be a victim of injustice, to stand up to a corrupt system and be killed by it. And, Christians believe, he did this to make atonement for our sins to free us from their penalty. Christians know, then, that, in the eyes of God, we were spiritually poor and powerless—we too were aliens and slaves, but God saved us by becoming oppressed for us.[9]

As a result of God's divine intervention in Jesus Christ—specifically, of his unjust crucifixion—we will receive the gifts of righteousness. The sins we confess will be forgiven. The sacrifices we made will be redeemed. The service we offered will be remembered. Best of all, by his resurrection from the dead we will have God's loving presence in our lives from here to eternity. The psalmist testified to this grace, giving us good words to pack with us on our spiritual climb:

9 Keller, *Making Sense of God*, 209–10.

I am continually with you;
 you hold my right hand.
You guide me with your counsel,
 and afterward you will receive me to glory. (vv. 23–24)

This is what the singer of Psalm 73 came to understand when he went to worship. He doesn't tell us exactly what he experienced that reminded him of God's final judgment. Maybe the Scripture he heard and the songs that he sang reminded him that God was holy, and he remembered that the holy God will do what is right. Or perhaps he saw flaming sacrifices offered on the great bronze altar in the temple courts, and this reminded him both that the wicked would be destroyed and that his sins would be forgiven. Whatever he saw, exactly, Asaph came away from worship with fresh confidence in the fairness of God and renewed hope in his salvation.

Not Slipping but Standing

Nearing the end of Psalm 73, Asaph realized how wrong he had been about the unrighteous. He also admitted how bad his attitude was about God. He confessed,

When my soul was embittered,
 when I was pricked in heart,
I was brutish and ignorant;
 I was like a beast toward you. (vv. 21–22)

Our bitter doubts about God are nothing to be proud of; they are sins to repent of.

Asaph also had a testimony to give. Knowing how the story ends strengthened his spiritual confidence so much that he closed the worship service with a personal confession of his faith. When by faith we see the end of our own story, we can make his words our own:

> Whom have I in heaven but you?
>> And there is nothing on earth that I desire besides you.
> My flesh and my heart may fail,
>> but God is the strength of my heart and my portion
>>> forever.

> For behold, those who are far from you shall perish;
>> you put an end to everyone who is unfaithful to you.
> But for me it is good to be near God;
>> I have made the Lord GOD my refuge,
>> that I may tell of all your works. (vv. 25–28)

Notice that Asaph returns to the pronouns "I" and "my," but not in a self-centered way. Now that he is back in the presence of God, there is a "you" in these verses too: his loving and faithful God. Because God is with him, Asaph is standing, not slipping. Rather than comprising all the things the wicked seem to have, his field of vision is filled with what *he* has, which happens to be the only thing he needs, or really wants, or could ever need: the loving presence of the living God.

Verse 28 contains a classic understatement: "But for me it is good to be near God." If God is good—which is where this psalm started—then what is good for us is to be where God is. The goodness of his loving presence is God's promise to us in Jesus Christ. The Savior who was born in the manger, was crucified at Calvary, was raised on Easter Sunday, and then ascended to glory has promised by his Spirit that he will never leave us or forsake us, but stay close beside us all the way. It is good for us to be near him today, and every day to follow, until the day he does for us what he did for the singer-songwriter of Psalm 73 and receives us into glory.

Why did I come out from the womb
to see toil and sorrow,
and spend my days in shame?

JEREMIAH 20:18

7

Doubting God's Loving Care

Jeremiah in Prison

IN A FAMOUS LYRIC from the sixteenth century, the Spanish mystic St. John of the Cross describes the soul's journey to God, who often seems to be shrouded in darkness. St. John's poem came to be known as "Dark Night of the Soul."

This title phrase has captured the imaginations of many saints and sinners. T. S. Eliot used it in his *Four Quartets*. Songwriters have set the line to music, including Van Morrison.[1] In "I Feel Loved," Depeche Mode sang of "the dark night of my soul" when "temptation's taking hold."[2] St. John's memorable phrase also shows up in Stephen King's thriller *Insomnia*. King borrowed it from the author F. Scott Fitzgerald, who wrote in his 1936 essay "The Crack-Up," "In a real dark night of the soul it is always three

1 See James Hirsen, "Dark Night of the Soul for America," Newsmax, November 23, 2020, https://www.newsmax.com/.

2 "I Feel Loved," by Martin Gore, track 2 on *Exciter*, Mute Records, 2001.

o'clock in the morning."[3] Flannery O'Connor wrote to a reader, "Right now the whole world seems to be going through a dark night of the soul."[4] Apparently, even cult novelist Douglas Adams knows this line, because he wrote a sci-fi adventure entitled *The Long Dark Tea-Time of the Soul*.[5]

There is a simple reason why Saint John's phrase has become so widely known: we all have dark nights of the soul. Eventually, everyone comes to a place of spiritual crisis, even bestselling authors and Grammy-winning songwriters. We have our doubts—we all do. Aspects of our life with God seem shrouded in mystery. And while this can happen during the daytime, it often happens during the dark hours of the night, when we are alone with our thoughts and wonder, *Is God there? Does God care?*

It Happened One Night

Apart from our Savior's sufferings on the cross, the clearest biblical example of a dark night of the soul comes from the life of Jeremiah. The poor prophet had been imprisoned. A man named Pashhur—who was the head of temple security and the chief of Israel's prophecy police—took exception to Jeremiah's message of judgment against Jerusalem. So he seized the prophet, beat him, and then bound him for the rest of the night.

The next day, Pashhur had a change of heart and removed Jeremiah's restraints. That morning the prophet opened a win-

3   F. Scott Fitzgerald, "The Crack-Up," with other collected essays in *The Crack-Up*, ed. Edmund Wilson (New York: New Directions, 1945), 75.

4   Flannery O'Connor to Betty Hester, September 6, 1955, American Reader, https://theamericanreader.com/, accessed November 27, 2023.

5   Douglas Adams, *The Long Dark Tea-Time of the Soul* (New York: Simon & Schuster, 1988).

dow to his soul. Jeremiah 20 records his thoughts and feelings after his long dark night of the soul. The prophet had been up all night, passing through what Dostoevsky called "the crucible of doubt."[6] In the light of a new day, he began to lament everything that was wrong with his life—as every believer does—including his frustration with the Almighty:

> O Lord, you have deceived me,
>   and I was deceived;
> you are stronger than I,
>   and you have prevailed. (v. 7)

Jeremiah had many reasons to be discouraged. To begin with, he was in danger. Because people hated his message of divine judgment, they were blaming him as the messenger, hoping to catch him making a false prophecy. Enemy priests gathered in the corners of the temple and pointed accusatory fingers in his direction. Verse 10 says:

> I hear many whispering.
>   Terror is on every side!
> "Denounce him! Let us denounce him!"
>   say all my close friends,
>   watching for my fall.
> "Perhaps he will be deceived;
>   then we can overcome him
>   and take our revenge on him."

---

6   Fyodor Dostoevsky, quoted in Christian Wiman, *My Bright Abyss: Meditation of a Modern Believer* (New York: Farrar, Straus and Giroux, 2013), 9.

Even Jeremiah's so-called friends were waiting for him to make a false move. He had already been beaten and put away in prison. There had been various death threats (see Jer. 11:18–21; 18:22–23). It was bad enough to be ostracized, but what would they do to him next?

The prophet was also discouraged because people were mocking him:

> I have become a laughingstock all the day;
> > everyone mocks me.
> For whenever I speak, I cry out,
> > I shout, "Violence and destruction!"
> For the word of the LORD has become for me
> > a reproach and derision all day long. (Jer. 20:7–8)

Evidently, Jerusalem's late-night comedians were getting their funniest material at Jeremiah's expense. His ministry was a joke; his message had become a punch line. "There goes that crazy old prophet," his tormentors said. "Did you hear what he did yesterday?" One insult was especially vicious. Critics mocked his prophecies of judgment by essentially calling him old "Terror on Every Side" (see Jer. 20:10). Verbal abuse may not seem very serious compared with a vicious beating, but eventually public ridicule starts to take its toll.

Jeremiah was despised and rejected. His friends betrayed him, even the closest of all friends. "O LORD," he lamented,

> *you* have deceived me,
> > and I was deceived. (Jer. 20:7)

Apparently, Jeremiah was starting to doubt whether God's word was true after all—Satan's oldest temptation, going back to the garden of Eden. God compelled Jeremiah to prophesy, and so he prophesied, but where was the judgment that God threatened? The longer God waited before fulfilling his word, the more Jeremiah wondered whether he had become a false prophet. Maybe God himself had lied to him—either by telling him the wrong thing to say or by promising to protect Jeremiah (see Jer. 1:8; 15:21) and then abandoning him to the wrath of his enemies.

Most of us can relate. Philosopher Mark Talbot says that in Jeremiah's terrible sufferings he went so far as "to malign God's character and, at least temporarily, abandon his faith and renounce his calling."[7] Even if we haven't gone that far, we still have our criticisms. We thought we understood God to say that he would do something for us, but he didn't do it. People have mocked us or criticized us. We felt like fools for believing what we believe about Jesus, or for speaking up on behalf of the word of God. Life has been so hard that we've started to wonder whether everything we have ever heard about the gospel is really true. During the long dark night when our souls have cried out to God, we haven't even been sure he listens. Or maybe we've been unable to pray at all. This was Tish Harrison Warren's experience, as she describes in her book *Prayer in the Night*: "I didn't know how to approach God anymore. There were too many things to say, too many questions without answers. My depth of pain overshadowed my ability with

---

7   Mark Talbot, *When the Stars Disappear: Help and Hope from Stories of Suffering in Scripture* (Wheaton, IL: Crossway, 2020), 34.

words. And, more painfully, I couldn't pray because I wasn't sure how to trust God."[8]

Even when we feel as if we cannot pray, we still wrestle with God. In his memoir *Telling Secrets*, the late novelist Frederick Buechner poses some of the doubtful questions that most Christians ask, whether by day or by night:

> Is the Lord at hand indeed? Many of us have believed in him for a long time, have also hungered to believe in him when with part of ourselves we sometimes couldn't believe in much of anything. In the midst of a suffering world and of our own small suffering, we have tried to believe in a God of love and power, the highest power beyond all others. Have we been right? Is it finally true what we have believed and hungered to believe?[9]

Take It to the Lord in Prayer

Jeremiah wrestled with similar questions during his long dark night of the soul. The poem he wrote about that experience shows us the single most important thing we can do when we have our doubts about God's loving care. Simply this: *talk to God about it*. Whatever doubts we have in the darkness, we should take them to the Lord in prayer.

Jeremiah 20 is the prayer of a suffering believer. Imagine the prophet in solitary confinement—weakened with physical pain, exhausted by emotional turmoil, fearful of what tomorrow might

---

8 Tish Harrison Warren, *Prayer in the Night: For Those Who Work or Watch or Weep* (Downers Grove, IL: InterVarsity Press, 2021), 12.

9 Frederick Buechner, *Telling Secrets: A Memoir* (1991; repr., New York: HarperOne, 2000), 103.

bring. Now hear the first words out of his mouth. They come in the form of an invocation to Almighty God. "O Lord," the prophet cries. "O Lord!" (v. 7).

God always invites us to take our troubles straight to him. This is what godly people have done throughout history. It is what Job did on the ash heap, when he was grieving the death of his loved ones (Job 1:21). It is what David did in the cave, when he was hiding from King Saul (Ps. 57). It is what Jonah did in the belly of the great fish, when he ran away from God (Jonah 2). It is also what Jesus did on the cross, when he was suffering for our sins and felt separated from his loving Father. "My God!" he cried out. "My God, my God" (Matt. 27:46).

Even when we think that God is the problem and not the solution, as Jeremiah did—even when we think he is incriminated by what we are experiencing—we should talk things over with him. In every dark night of the soul, we should take our troubles to the secret place and meet with God in prayer. Where else can we open our hearts so freely? Who else could possibly address our concerns? There is never any need for us to hide our feelings. We can always take our struggles to the Lord in prayer.

Praying and Praising in Prison

Something amazing happened to Jeremiah as he prayed that night in prison: he began to take heart. Somehow, the Holy Spirit was ministering to his soul. Suddenly—and totally unexpectedly—he interrupted his complaint long enough to hold a short worship service. Yes, he felt alone and afraid, depressed and discouraged. Yes, he believed in that moment that God was against him. Nevertheless, in Jeremiah 20:11–13 he offers a little song of praise to his God. This gives us a second thing to do in the dark nights of our soul, however counterintuitive it may seem: *give praise to God.*

Jeremiah's worship service may have been short, but it was also complete. His psalm includes a confession of faith, a petition for deliverance, and a hymn of praise.

The prophet's confession of faith reads like this:

> But the LORD is with me as a dread warrior;
>> therefore my persecutors will stumble;
>> they will not overcome me.
> They will be greatly shamed,
>> for they will not succeed.
> Their eternal dishonor
>> will never be forgotten. (v. 11)

Jeremiah did not understand what was happening to him. Even God seemed to be against him. Yet the prophet still testified to what he knew to be true about the character of his Savior. In his comments on these verses, John Calvin wrote:

> Here the Prophet sets up God's aid against all the plottings formed against him. However, then, might perfidious friends on one hand try privately to entrap him, and open enemies might on the other hand publicly oppose him, he yet doubted not but that God would be a sufficient protection to him.[10]

10 John Calvin, *A Commentary on Jeremiah*, 5 vols. (Edinburgh: Banner of Truth, 1989), 3:38.

Jeremiah believed that God was with him even when God seemed far away. Jeremiah knew that the Lord was strong even though Jeremiah felt powerless. He expected his enemies to be defeated even though they appeared to triumph. So, even when he was tempted to doubt it, the prophet confessed that God would be his salvation.

What is the functional confession of our own faith—not just the creed we recite in church but the confidence we live by every day? Despite our troubles, are we able to say that God is with us like a mighty warrior?

Next comes prayer. Deep down, Jeremiah believed in God's loving care, and because of this, he was willing to ask for help:

> O LORD of hosts, who tests the righteous,
>   who sees the heart and the mind,
> let me see your vengeance upon them,
>   for to you have I committed my cause. (v. 12)

When Jeremiah doubted, he did not try to solve his problems on his own. Instead, he committed his cause to the Lord. For him, this meant praying that his cause would be vindicated. Our case may be different, but the principle is the same: if we believe that God is with us and has the power to help us, then we should ask him for the help that only he can give.

Earlier I mentioned Tish Harrison Warren's book *Prayer in the Night*. Warren wrote the book in part because she wanted to reacquaint the contemporary church with Compline, the ancient nighttime prayer preserved for us in the Book of Common Prayer. What we need in the middle of the night, she writes, is a way to experience "the vast mystery of God, the surety of God's power, the reassurance of God's goodness."[11] Compline grants us these experiences through its consoling petitions:

> Keep watch, dear Lord, with those who work, or watch, or weep this night, and give your angels charge over those who sleep. Tend the sick, Lord Christ; give rest to the weary, bless the dying, soothe the suffering, pity the afflicted, shield the joyous; and all for your love's sake. *Amen.*

Despite his doubts, Jeremiah began to believe so strongly that he added praise to prayer and closed his worship time with a hymn. Like Paul and Silas in prison (Acts 16:25), the prophet burst into song:

> Sing to the LORD;
>   praise the LORD!
> For he has delivered the life of the needy
>   from the hand of evildoers. (Jer. 20:13)

Imagine Jeremiah bent over in the stocks as he sings. He may not have had enough breath to sing a long anthem, but he could manage at least one short song of praise. The prophet had come through his doubts to a place of such confidence in the Lord that he praised God *during* his dark night of the soul. Notice how this little psalm refers to the needy person in the singular. Literally, the Lord rescues the life "of the needy one" (v. 13), meaning the

---

11 Warren, *Prayer in the Night*, 7.

prophet himself. When we say that Jesus saves, we mean that he sees us personally and rescues us individually, as part of a redeemed humanity.

Like Jeremiah, Dietrich Bonhoeffer was imprisoned for the sake of God's word. Bonhoeffer endured the dark night of his soul in a Nazi concentration camp. Yet, even there, the brave theologian did not stop praising God but worshiped him the way Jeremiah did. Listen to these words from one of the Bonhoeffer's most famous prayers from prison:

> I am lonely, but you do not abandon me. . . .
> I am restless, but with you is peace. . . .
> I do not understand your ways, but you know [the] right
>   way for me.[12]

It is always good to praise the Lord, even when we have our doubts about his loving care. During one of my own dark nights, I wrote a hymn to express my thoughts and feelings to God. The opening stanza ends with a question:

> Jesus, hear me in the darkness—hear this dying sinner's plea:
> All I've done is empty, worthless—there is nothing good in me!
> Lonely in my desperation, will You come and rescue me?

Notice that these words come in the form of a prayer, which is one half of a conversation with God. The best thing to do when we are depressed and discouraged is go to worship. Keep confessing,

---

12 Dietrich Bonhoeffer, *Dietrich Bonhoeffer Works*, vol. 8, *Letters and Papers from Prison* (Minneapolis: Augsburg Fortress, 2009), 195.

keep praying, keep singing. Even when we have a complaint to make, we are called to confess our faith in God, pray for deliverance, and then praise his name.

A Surprise Ending

It is tempting to stop right there, with Jeremiah's psalm of praise, but that is not how the story ends. We take the Bible as it comes, and this time—spoiler alert!—it ends on a huge downer. Before the last note of the prophet's praise song fades away, he tells us that he just wants to die:

> Cursed be the day
>   on which I was born!
> The day when my mother bore me,
>   let it not be blessed!
> Cursed be the man who brought the news to my father,
> "A son is born to you,"
>   making him very glad.
> Let that man be like the cities
>   that the Lord overthrew without pity;
> let him hear a cry in the morning
>   and an alarm at noon,
> because he did not kill me in the womb;
>   so my mother would have been my grave,
>   and her womb forever great. (Jer. 20:14–17)

These may be the bitterest curses in the Bible. Just when we thought that Jeremiah was overcoming his doubts, he had what Mark Talbot calls an absolute "crisis of faith" that plunged him into "life-cursing despair."[13] This was the low point of Jeremiah's ministry, in which he did some of the same things we are tempted to do when life seems to go against us: he blamed God, rejected his calling, and cursed the day he was born.

Instead of celebrating his birthday, Jeremiah condemned it. He wanted to reach back into history and damn everyone who had anything to do with his birth. In particular, he wished that the man who brought his father the "good news" had strangled him in his infancy instead.

Jeremiah's mood swung from praising to cursing with dizzying speed. One verse is a psalm of high praise; the next is a lament of utter despair. This has led some scholars to conclude that verse 14 "can hardly belong after verse 13."[14] They view chapter 20 as a hodgepodge of the prophet's sayings. Even John Calvin is mystified; to him it seems "unworthy of the holy man to pass suddenly from thanksgiving to God into imprecations, as though he had forgotten himself."[15]

Perhaps Jeremiah *had* forgotten himself, but these verses do belong together. They may not belong together by logic, but who says the life of the soul is always logical? Jeremiah's curses followed his praises because that was the way it was during his long dark night of the soul. Sometimes prayer doesn't make everything all better, especially right away. Sometimes it only seems to make things worse. Sometimes we go from complaining to praying and back to cursing. The Bible doesn't shy away from this confusion,

---

13 Talbot, *When the Stars Disappear*, 32, 38.

14 R. E. O. White, *The Indomitable Prophet: A Biographical Commentary on Jeremiah* (Grand Rapids, MI: Eerdmans, 1992), 162.

15 Calvin, *Commentary on Jeremiah*, 3:44.

even in the lives of the greatest saints. Commenting on Jeremiah 20, Derek Kidner writes, "Together with other tortured cries from [Jeremiah] and his fellow sufferers, these raw wounds in Scripture remain lest we forget the sharpness of the age-long struggle, or the frailty of the finest overcomers."[16]

Notice that Jeremiah stopped short of cursing God, or his parents, perhaps because he knew these were both capital offenses in Israel (Lev. 20:9; 24:13–16). He also stopped short of suicide, although in this black moment he did wonder if his life had any purpose. Like many desperate souls, he asked the question that closes Jeremiah 20:

> Why did I come out from the womb
>   to see toil and sorrow,
> and spend my days in shame? (v. 18)

When Suffering Hands You a Question Mark

Jeremiah's dark night of the soul put a giant question mark over his existence. He had known the suffering of physical torture, the shame of public humiliation, and the sorrow of watching people turn their backs on God. Even though he was strong in faith, there were times when he had more questions than answers. In his spiritual darkness, he doubted everything: his creation, his salvation, his vocation.[17] He just wanted to quit, as many people in ministry do. According to one recent study, more than 60 percent

---

16 Derek Kidner, *The Message of Jeremiah: Against Wind and Tide*, The Bible Speaks Today (Downers Grove, IL: InterVarsity Press, 1987), 81.

17 J. G. McConville, *Judgment and Promise: An Interpretation of the Book of Jeremiah* (Leicester, UK: Apollos, 1993), 73–74.

of all Christian leaders "give up far too early, lose their faith, mess up, and fall deep."[18]

We should find hope in the fact that although Jeremiah 20 ends with a question mark, this punctuation mark does not in fact get the last word. By definition, someone who is in a dark night of the soul cannot see the light. But morning will dawn. Chapter 21 thus begins with a fresh word from God, which Jeremiah faithfully proclaims. The prophet lived to preach another day. In fact, as his ministry went forward, he became a prophet of hope for all nations—the one who famously testified,

> The steadfast love of the LORD never ceases;
>   his mercies never come to an end;
> they are new every morning;
>   great is your faithfulness. (Lam. 3:22–23)

If we step back to see the bigger biblical picture, we get a good answer to the question that the prophet left dangling at the end of Jeremiah 20. Why *did* he come out of the womb to see trouble and sorrow? God answered this question back in chapter 1, when he called the prophet to ministry. Jeremiah needed to be reminded of the first thing that God ever said to him:

> Before I formed you in the womb I knew you,
> and before you were born I consecrated you;
> I appointed you a prophet to the nations. (Jer. 1:5)

---

18 Evi Rodemann, "Befriending Pain in Leadership: Why Crisis Lets Us Grow as Leaders," Lausanne Movement, July 22, 2022, https://lausanne.org/about/blog/befriending-pain-in-leadership.

When Jeremiah traced his troubles back to the womb, he didn't go back far enough! God traced his promises back even further, to the time before Jeremiah was conceived. God had a purpose for Jeremiah—as he has a purpose for us—that goes back before the beginning of time. Like the prophet Jeremiah, God set us apart for salvation and for ministry from all eternity.

The Bible says that "he [God] chose us in him [Jesus] before the foundation of the world" (Eph. 1:4). God also set us apart to do his work in the world. "We are his workmanship," the Bible says, "created in Christ Jesus for good works, which God prepared beforehand, that we should walk in them" (Eph. 2:10). Even when trouble places a giant question mark over our existence, God's loving plan for us and his grace for us in Jesus Christ always have the last word.

I am reminded of the testimony of Wheaton College alumnus Andrew Brunson, who, for his testimony of faith in Christ, languished in a Turkish prison for 735 days—most of it in solitary confinement.[19] Brunson suffered terribly there, not only physically and emotionally but also spiritually. He writes:

> My two years in prison were marked by what I would call the silence of God, and not having any sense of His presence. . . . To have that intimacy removed led to a fence around my heart toward God.

---

19 The account that follows—including the quotations—comes from Andrew Brunson's interview with Lindy Lowry, "Why Andrew Brunson Never Heard from God in Prison," September 7, 2021, https://www.opendoorsusa.org/; see Sam Storms, Enjoy God (blog), April 27, 2022, https://www.samstorms.org/enjoying-god-blog/post/why -andrew-brunson-never-heard-from-god-in-prison.

I broke physically. . . . I broke emotionally. I went into that spiritual crisis.

Brunson testifies further that in his first year of confinement he was too wounded to sing "Great Is Thy Faithfulness." But eventually God put a song in his heart. "It wasn't as much a breakthrough," he says, as

> a shifting that led to a rebuilding. And that was a decision on my part to lay aside my conditions and expectations of God and simply be faithful to Him. So, I said: "Whatever You do or don't do, I will follow You. If You do not give Your voice, I'll still follow. If You don't give me Your presence, I'll still follow You. If You do not set me free, I'll still be faithful. I'm going to fight for my relationship with You and I choose to turn my eyes 'toward' rather than 'away.' "
>
> In my weakness, at the bottom of my pit, I knew I might only be able to turn slightly in His direction, but even if I turned one degree toward Him, that was all the difference in the world than turning one degree away.

Our Savior did the same thing when he was crucified, and there was a giant question mark hanging over his cross. He said, "My God, my God, why have you forsaken me?" (Matt. 27:46). When heaven refused to answer, Jesus had to live with the question, and die with it too, because he didn't really get an answer until three days later, when he rose again. But our Savior *did* get an answer. The resurrection was the Father's *yes* to the Son's atoning sacrifice for our sins and the proof that Jesus was not forsaken in the end, but lovingly raised to everlasting glory.

As a doubter and as a believer—as a doubter-believer—living today with huge question marks, don't stop talking to God, do start worshiping again, and then let the empty tomb have the last word.

*And Jesus said to him, "'If you can'! All things are possible
for one who believes." Immediately the father of the
child cried out and said, "I believe; help my unbelief!"*

MARK 9:23–24

8

Doubting God's Miraculous Healing

The Father in the Crowd

IS ANY PRAYER MORE DESPERATE than a parent's plea for the healing of a beloved child?

One African couple prayed for the healing of their beautiful daughter Ella, who was born with a heart defect that limited her oxygen flow to 70 percent. Local doctors said that nothing could be done to help her and doubted she would live past age five. Her parents took her to a large hospital in a neighboring country. There they learned about possible heart surgery, but only if they could go overseas to get it. When their travel visa was denied, they were heartbroken. They tried to pray in faith, but still they wondered, *Would Ella ever be healed?*

A Boy beyond Help

If anyone in the Bible could relate to this family's distress, it would be the father we meet in Mark 9—a desperate man who stood out from the crowd one day to ask if there was any way Jesus could heal his son.

Frankly, the man had his doubts. Jesus's disciples had already tried to help and completely failed. He explained to Jesus: "Teacher, I brought my son to you, for he has a spirit that makes him mute. And whenever it seizes him, it throws him down, and he foams and grinds his teeth and becomes rigid. So I asked your disciples to cast it out, and they were not able" (vv. 17–18).

By this point in the Gospel of Mark, Jesus had given his disciples the authority to cast out demons (3:15; 6:7), and they had performed many miraculous healings as a result (6:13). Yet this time they were unable to make a difference. Why was this? In Matthew's account, the disciples privately asked Jesus the same question: "Why could we not cast it out?" Jesus said to them: "Because of your little faith" (Matt. 17:19–20). This gives us another good reason to fight against unbelief: our lack of faith will hinder or even prevent our effective ministry to people in need.

Various scholars have noted that the boy's symptoms sound similar to epilepsy.[1] Yet there was also a spiritual dimension. This was a difficult case of demonic possession. We know this because an "unclean spirit" is mentioned throughout the passage. The healing the lad needed, therefore, was spiritual as well as physical. Simply put, he needed an exorcism. The noisy crowd could see this for themselves. When they brought the boy to Jesus, and "the spirit saw him, immediately it convulsed the boy, and he fell on the ground and rolled about, foaming at the mouth" (Mark 9:20).

---

1   For example, see William L. Lane, *The Gospel of Mark*, New International Commentary on the New Testament (Grand Rapids, MI: Eerdmans, 1974), 331.

Jesus then inquired about the boy's medical case history. "How long has this been happening to him?" he asked. He did not ask this question to make a better diagnosis, in all likelihood, but to help the boy's father verbalize his need. The desperate man answered by saying: "From childhood. And it has often cast him into fire and into water, to destroy him" (Mark 9:21–22).

Whatever the boy's precise medical and spiritual condition may have been, it was lifelong. Also, it was potentially fatal, and thus the father was afraid of losing his son. The Bible rightly describes the devil as someone who "prowls around like a roaring lion, seeking someone to devour" (1 Pet. 5:8). If Satan could, he would destroy us, body and soul. This is one of the reasons we all need healing—physical, spiritual, and psychological healing. It is harmful for us to live in this fallen world. Sooner or later, we all need renewal for our weary souls, comfort for our grieving hearts, healing for our broken bodies. In this sinful world, we are truly harmed by what others have done, both personally and communally. Behind it all is the homicidal enemy who has been hurting humanity since the garden of Eden—the evil devil who, with murderous intent, wants to destroy our very personhood.

Anyone who has ever felt sick or wounded can empathize with this poor family and how powerless they felt. The failure of the disciples only added to the father's sense of desperation. By the time Jesus arrived, people were arguing with one another, as we often do when there is a problem no one can solve.

Evidently, the disciples were in way over their heads. We can relate to this as well. It is not just our own need for healing that makes us feel powerless and sometimes doubtful about what God will do. We are also burdened and sometimes overwhelmed by the needs of people we are trying to help. We watch someone we love struggle with an unending illness. We try to comfort someone who is inconsolable. We pray for someone to get better, only to watch him or her get worse. Then we wonder how we and our loved ones will ever be healed. Is there any hope?

If You Can!

Sometimes it feels as if the healing we need will take a miracle. This was true in Mark 9, as Keith Johnson explains:

> The father needed a miracle. His son had a spiritual affliction that often left him on the ground, seized up, and foaming at the mouth. The terror could strike at any moment. Once, his son had been standing next to the fire and then fell into it, causing terrible scars. Another time he was cast into the water and nearly drowned. The father worried about his son constantly, and he rarely let him stray from his sight. No doctor had been able to help. Maybe Jesus could do something.[2]

Yes, maybe Jesus *could* do something. This was the father's only hope. Yet when Jesus arrived on the scene, he too seemed frustrated. This was one of those poignant moments in the Gospels when our Savior felt weighed down by the troubles of fallen humanity. "O faithless generation," he said wearily, "how long

---

2   Keith Johnson, "Doubt," in *Life Questions Every Student Asks: Faithful Responses to Common Issues*, ed. Gary M. Burge and David Lauber (Downers Grove, IL: InterVarsity Press, 2020), 127.

am I to be with you? How long am I to bear with you?" (v. 19). Jesus was disappointed by their disbelief.

Rather than waiting for an answer to his rhetorical questions, Jesus issued a thrilling invitation: "Bring him to me" (v. 19). This simple welcome marked the turning point in the boy's life. Today it gives genuine hope to anyone who needs healing. Whenever the people we care about need help, we are invited to do what the father in the crowd did and bring them to Jesus. We do this by showing them selfless love and praying for what they need. We can do the same thing with our own problems, whatever they happen to be. "Bring them to me," Jesus says, in effect. "Bring me your anxiety about the future. Bring me your stress over all the things that could go wrong. Bring me your chronic illness. Bring your broken relationships and the abuse you have suffered. Bring me your disappointment in life and your life-dominating addiction. Bring me any trouble you have, no matter how big, no matter how small."

The father in Mark 9 *did* bring his boy to Jesus. This was the precise moment when the evil spirit took control and sent the poor child into convulsions. What could possibly be done to help? Only something that Jesus could do. And so, "with courage born of desperation," as Keith Johnson describes it," the father asked Jesus to heal his son.[3]

Notice the man's prayer: "*If* you can do anything, have compassion on us and help us" (v. 22). There are several positives here. The father does bring his boy to Jesus. He does appeal to the compassion of the loving Son of God. In fact, he does something

3   Johnson, "Doubt," 128.

he has never done before and asks Jesus to help, and this is the most important thing we can do whenever someone needs healing.

The problem was the conditional term at the beginning of the man's petition. Jesus thought that the little word "if" betrayed a disturbing lack of confidence in his power to heal. "If you can!" Jesus exclaimed. "All things are possible for one who believes" (v. 23).

How did Jesus say this? What was his body language and tone of voice? Was he indignant? Exasperated? Or did he say it with a slightly raised eyebrow and a twinkle in his eye? "If you can?" Jesus queried. The worried father had come face-to-face with the Creator of the universe, who scattered the stars across the evening sky and first breathed life into our spongy lungs. The man was in the presence of the miracle worker who made the lame to walk and the blind to see. He was speaking with God the Son Almighty, who within his own divine being possesses the fullness of omnipotence. And still he had the temerity to say to this great Savior, "If you can"?

Jesus had every right to take offense at the man's uncertainty and unbelief, yet he responded instead with good humor. There are no *ifs* when it comes to the healing power of the Lord Jesus Christ. He is able to perform healing miracles, and it is absurd for anyone to think otherwise.

Help My Unbelief!

This brings us to the most relatable moment in Mark's account. When Jesus said, "All things are possible for one who believes" (9:23), the father in the crowd almost believed it. The first words out of his mouth formed a confession of his faith: "I believe." But apparently, he couldn't quite believe it, because without pausing for breath he also cried out, "Help my unbelief!" (9:24).

Like many of the best people we meet in the Bible—and like most of us—this man was a doubter-believer. He was caught somewhere between faith and skepticism, in what Philip Yancey calls "the borderlands of belief."[4] He *did* believe. He believed in Jesus enough to bring his child for healing, enough to see the Savior's compassion, enough to pray for greater faith. But he also found it hard to believe, which is why he said, "If you can," and asked Jesus to help his "unbelief." There is a double prayer here: a prayer for healing and a prayer for faith. The man believed enough to ask for a miracle and at the same time doubted enough to know that he needed help with his unbelief.

There is such a thing, of course, as active denial of the central truths of the Christian faith. An unbeliever in this sense is someone who refuses to believe in the truth of the Bible, or the deity of Jesus Christ, or the salvation he offers through his atoning death and bodily resurrection. Such unbelief is sin, which is why we need to wrestle with our doubts rather than giving in to them. The Bible is clear: unbelievers who deny the gospel will not inherit the kingdom of God (Rev. 21:8). The writer to the Hebrews thus gives us this life-saving warning: "Take care, brothers, lest there be in any of you an evil, unbelieving heart, leading you to fall away from the living God" (Heb. 3:12).

That is not the kind of unbelief that Mark 9 is talking about, however. The man we meet here believed and also struggled to believe. If this seems like a contradiction, then we need to

---

4   Philip Yancey, *A Skeptic's Guide to Faith: What It Takes to Make the Leap* (Grand Rapids, MI: Zondervan, 2009), 19.

recognize that faith and doubt often go together. Christian Wiman describes this paradox in a short essay about his ongoing spiritual uncertainty, where he writes:

> I always have this sense that something is going to resolve my spiritual anxieties once and for all, that one day I'll just relax and be a believer. I read book after book. I seek out intense experiences in art, in nature, or in conversations with people I respect and who seem to rest more securely in their faith than I do. Sometimes it seems that gains are made, for these can and do provide relief and instruction. But always the anxiety comes back, is the norm from which faith deviates, if faith is even what you could call these intense but somehow vague and fleeting experiences of God.[5]

Perhaps an analogy will help to clarify our spiritual struggle. Faith and doubt are not like the on and off alternatives of a toggle switch but are more like settings on a dimmer switch. Sometimes our faith burns bright. Sometimes it grows dim. What we see in Mark 9:24, therefore, is something familiar to all of us: the flickering of faith and doubt. Keith Johnson describes this father as a man who "stands in the place of every believer, because the entire Christian life occurs within the dynamic of faith and doubt."[6] Where do we stand at this moment in the dynamic between faith and doubt? And what would it take for the Holy Spirit to brighten our belief?

5 Christian Wiman, *My Bright Abyss: Meditation of a Modern Believer* (New York: Farrar, Straus and Giroux, 2013), 107.
6 Johnson, "Doubt," 129.

As he fiddled with the dimmer switch in his soul, the desperate father did the best thing he could possibly do and asked Jesus for help. Concerning his request—"Lord, I believe; help my unbelief"—Frederick Buechner observes that such a prayer "is the best any of us can do really, but thank God it is enough."[7] In our ongoing struggle with doubt, we should never forget that the help only Jesus can give is never more than a prayer away, as we have seen more than once in our study of biblical doubters. The proximity of faith through prayer is the valuable conclusion that Johnson reaches in his reflection on the place of doubt in the Christian life. He writes:

> Doubt is not the opposite of faith. Doubt often is simply the form faith takes as Christians venture beyond the limits of their comprehension. It is not necessarily a sign of disobedience. Rather, doubt often results directly from a believer's obedience to the command to "take every thought captive" to Christ. This does not mean that doubt should be taken lightly or embraced. Christians always should be moving from doubt toward confidence. But that journey can be long and difficult, perhaps even lasting a lifetime. And it is a journey that requires help from Christ. The father's words belong to every Christian: "I believe; help my unbelief!"[8]

7 Frederick Buechner, *The Magnificent Defeat* (New York: HarperCollins, 1985), 35.
8 Johnson, "Doubt," 129; later, on p. 134, Johnson writes: "The Bible does not encourage believers to embrace doubt, but it does not always condemn doubt as sinful. Instead, doubt is depicted as a product of the frailty that comes with being a finite and fallen human being." See also C. S. Lewis, "On Obstinacy of Belief," in *The World's Last Night and Other Essays* (New York: Harcourt, Brace, 1960), 13–30.

If faith were something we could manage to conjure on our own, such a prayer would be unnecessary. But the Bible never describes faith as something that comes from somewhere inside us; it always defines faith as a gift from God. The apostle Paul famously said: "For by grace you have been saved through faith. And this is not your own doing; it is the gift of God" (Eph. 2:8). If this is true—that faith is a divine gift—then the very best thing to do when we doubt is ask Jesus to help us believe. The words "help my unbelief" may "feel like an admission of guilt, like a statement of failure," writes Barnabas Piper. Yet to pray this way at all, he goes on to say, is a remarkable announcement that we *do* believe![9]

Our Savior has all the sympathy in the world for people with honest doubts who have a genuine desire for faith and thus ask him to help them believe. Jesus is the living proof of Jude verse 22, which instructs us to "have mercy on those who doubt." Our Savior will show us the same mercy when we ask him for the gift of faith.

Admittedly, sometimes prayer is exactly the problem, because one of our biggest doubts is whether God really does hear us and answer us. In a study of American spirituality, the Pew Research Center discovered that

most skeptics have no experiential relationship to prayer. When Christians talk about the "power of prayer," skeptics have no real connection to anyone or anything on the "other

---

9   Barnabas Piper, *Help My Unbelief: Why Doubt Is Not the Enemy of Faith* (Charlotte: Good Book, 2020), 78.

end," believing that their words, no matter how earnest, remain unheard.[10]

The truth is that God hears our prayers—he always does. Because God is patient, he may not answer our prayers right away. And he may not answer them the way we would answer them, because he has bigger purposes in mind. But if there is one petition God loves to answer, it is a genuine request for the help we need in order to believe. When we struggle with doubt—as most people do—we should pray specifically for the gift of faith. We should pray the way the desperate father essentially did in the Gospel of Mark: "Lord Jesus, I do believe. But when I don't believe, help my unbelief!" This prayer, writes Barnabas Piper,

> should be the daily cry of every Christian. It is the cry of someone in the depths of despair who has only enough belief to say that prayer. And it is the cry of the fire-filled preacher before standing in the pulpit on Sunday morning. It is the cry of the mother who is running out of patience with her children and the businessman who is just a couple of clicks away from viewing porn. It is the cry of the person who is spiritually dry and has no desire to open her Bible and the person who has devoured all of Romans and is starting on 1 Corinthians just this morning. It is the cry of the sinner caught in an affair who deeply yearns to repent, to leave behind his shameful ways and be whole in Jesus and in marriage.

10 "25% of Americans Are Skeptical about Christianity. Why Is This So Important?," CT Creative Studio, March 14, 2022, https://www.christianitytoday.com/partners/he-gets-us/insights-into-skeptics.html.

It is a confession of need. It is a celebration of hope. It is the full scope of a life of faith.[11]

Waking Up Healed

What happens to people who struggle with spiritual doubt? Happily, the most likely outcome is that their faith grows stronger. Here the research is more encouraging. A study by the Barna Group reveals that two-thirds of American adults who self-identify as Christians say they have gone through periods when they "questioned what they believe about religion or God." Sadly, some of them ended up walking away from God, which is why it is so important for us to fight for our faith. But eventually the vast majority of Christians who find it hard to believe come back stronger than ever.[12] Praise God!

This is what Christian Wiman discovered when he struggled with doubt—honest spiritual doubt. Wiman admitted that his doubts were deeply painful, but he also testified that they purified his soul. "Far beneath" the doubt, he wrote, "no matter how severe its drought, how thoroughly your skepticism seems to have salted the ground of your soul, faith, durable faith, is steadily taking root."[13]

This must be what happened to the man we read about in Mark chapter 9. After a flicker of doubt, the desperate father saw Jesus answer his prayers by healing his son. The way Jesus did it was dramatic. The crowd was growing. More and more people came running up to see what was happening. Then Jesus "rebuked the unclean spirit, saying to it, 'You mute and deaf spirit, I command

11 Piper, *Help My Unbelief*, 79–80.
12 Michael Hakmin Lee, "No Longer Christian," *Outreach*, January/February 2022, 49.
13 Wiman, *My Bright Abyss*, 76.

you, come out of him and never enter him again'" (v. 25). At first people thought this made the situation worse. After "crying out and convulsing him terribly," the demon came out, but "the boy was like a corpse," so most of them said, "He is dead" (v. 26).

This apparent setback turned out to be an adumbration of the resurrection—a foreshadowing. Back in verse 10, the disciples had asked Jesus what he meant when he started talking to them about "rising from the dead." Well, here was a glimpse of his resurrection power, because Jesus simply took the boy "by the hand and lifted him up, and he arose" (v. 27). For the rest of his life, the boy would be able to say, "Up from the ground, I arose!" And his father would testify that even when he doubted, God was faithful. The man had done the right thing when he brought his son to Jesus. The father's faith—doubtful though it was—was well-placed. His son was healed.

The resurrection, which is merely hinted at in chapter 9, came to glorious fulfillment at the end of Mark's Gospel, when certain women arrived at the tomb of the crucified Christ and "saw that the stone had been rolled back" (16:4). Our Savior's glorious life after his atoning death is the ground of all our hopes for healing. We may not be healed yet, but one day we will be. We have this hope because we trust in the risen Christ. In her consoling book *Prayer in the Night*, Tish Harrison Warren finds future hope in the once-and-for-all resurrection of Jesus Christ:

> The Christian story proclaims that our ultimate hope doesn't lie in our lifetime, in making life work for us on this side of the grave. We watch and wait for "the resurrection of the dead and the life of the world to come." God's promise to make all

things new will not be fulfilled till God breaks into time, bearing eternity in his wake.

Christians believe that this cosmic reordering has already begun in the resurrection of Christ. Jesus' resurrection is the sole evidence that love triumphs over death, that beauty outlives horror, that the meek will inherit the earth, that those who mourn will be comforted. The reason I can continue watching and waiting, even as the world is shrouded in darkness, is because the things I long for are not rooted in wishful thinking or religious ritual but are as solid as a stone rolled away.[14]

The story Mark tells about the father in the crowd and his demon-possessed son gives us doubt-conquering hope for our own eventual healing. By the power of his empty tomb, Jesus Christ has authority over the demons that torment our souls, over the dark emotions that threaten to overwhelm us, over the diseases that debilitate us, over wounds so deep that we are afraid to let anyone touch them. At the end of this story, Jesus said something to his disciples that applies to so many of our own painful struggles: "This kind cannot be driven out by anything but prayer" (9:29). We can try everything imaginable to dull the pain, but eventually we discover that nothing in the entire world is as powerful as prayer in the name of the risen Christ.

When we pray, Jesus heals. This does not mean, of course, that God will heal us right away, or even that he will heal everything during this lifetime. The healing in Mark 9 is not a promise of

14 Tish Harrison Warren, *Prayer in the Night: For Those Who Work or Watch or Weep* (Downers Grove, IL: InterVarsity Press, 2021), 57.

our immediate deliverance; it is a sign of the coming kingdom of God, when at last every sorrow will be consoled, every pain removed, and every tear wiped away.

We need to wait for our full healing. There is a vivid picture of this in *The Lord of the Rings*, by J. R. R. Tolkien. Through his heroic journey to Mount Doom, Frodo Baggins helps rescue Middle-earth from the tyranny of Sauron. Afterward, he is rescued by eagles and carried to the Houses of Healing, where he is nursed back to health by skilled and loving care. But Frodo still bears visible scars from being stabbed and bitten. His soul remains tormented by the unspeakable evils he has suffered. He bears a weariness that he will never be able to unburden. What Frodo needs is a deeper healing than this world can ever give him. And so, in the end, he must leave Middle-earth and sail across the sea to the Undying Lands.

Each of us has a similar journey to make. It will be sad to leave this old world behind. But when we wake up and see Jesus, we will be healed. Life after death means comfort for all our sorrows and healing from all our pain.

Maybe Ella could tell us what this is like. I mentioned her sad medical situation at the beginning of this chapter. The poor girl needed open heart surgery, but she was blocked from getting it. Happily, Ella's father received a Billy Graham Scholarship to attend the Wheaton College Graduate School. When he matriculated, his family had permission to travel to the United States, and when they arrived, they discovered that they were eligible for Medicaid. Soon Ella was wheeled into the surgical suite at one of the best hospitals in Chicago, all expenses paid.

Imagine the almost miraculous moment at her hospital bed when Ella first opened her eyes, looked at her mother and father, realized that she was still alive, and heard that her surgery was totally successful. Her heart was healed!

Through the gift of sometimes doubtful yet genuine faith in Jesus Christ, one day we will open our eyes to the light of heaven's eternal day. We will realize that we are alive again and discover that we are totally healed—body, soul, and spirit. Lord, help us to believe this!

Then [Jesus] said to Thomas, "Put your finger here, and see my hands; and put out your hand, and place it in my side. Do not disbelieve, but believe."

JOHN 20:27

9

Doubting God's Resurrection Power

Thomas in the Upper Room

DOES ANYTHING CAUSE more spiritual doubt than the cold finality of death?

Taisiia Lukich sank into doubt and despair following the terrible loss she suffered after Russia invaded Ukraine in February of 2022.[1] She and her boyfriend had been talking about a wedding that year. But when the Russians invaded, Taisiia became a refugee and Alex went off to fight with the Ukrainian army.

When Taisiia didn't hear from Alex for several days, she started to worry, though she wasn't surprised. "It was not the first time he didn't answer me for a long time," she said, "because, you know,

---

1 Taisiia's story, summarized in what follows, is told in Sarah Eekhoff Zylstra, "One Year Later, Christians in Ukraine Say, 'We Wouldn't Want to Be Anywhere Else,'" TGC, February 24, 2023, https://www.thegospelcoalition.org/.

there are a lot of broken internet and cell phone connections." Four days later, one of Alex's friends told her not to call or text again: her fiancé had been killed in combat.

In the days that followed, Taisiia came undone. She stopped eating or drinking or sleeping. Because his body had been disfigured, Alex's casket was closed for the funeral, which made Taisiia wonder if he was really inside. Furious with God, she stopped reading her Bible. When she prayed, her words were angry. "I felt like I was falling into a pit," she later wrote—a pit "of grief and sorrow and crying and pain. I felt like I had no future anymore, that there was no reason to live my life."

But even when she lost the will to live, Taisiia kept reaching out to the God she doubted. "One day," she testified, "when I no longer had the strength to endure what was going on inside of me, I prayed, asking God for all that love and peace and comfort he had for me." Taisiia fell asleep crying, but as soon as she woke up, she knew that she had been renewed. It felt like a miracle!

Later, as she reflected on her experience of life after death, Taisiia wrote:

Often in difficult situations we pay attention only to the pain this world has given us. We forget to look at Christ, who knew from the beginning of the centuries this pain would be in our lives. He has already prepared comfort for us precisely for these situations. God gave comfort in that moment where I stopped hoping that I would ever have comfort. I was so shut up in my desperate thoughts that I forgot that God gave up his Son.

We should never forget that God gave up his Son for us on the cross. Nor should we ever forget that God brought him back from the grave by the power of the Holy Spirit. Jesus is not dead but alive! His resurrection is the source of God's life-renewing work in our souls, even when death causes us to doubt his saving power.

Doubting Thomas

Sometimes it is hard for us to believe in life after death. The true Bible story that shows this perhaps most clearly is the story of "Doubting Thomas," as he is usually called. I prefer to think of him as Believing Thomas, but he did have his doubts.

Most of us would have shared the man's skepticism. Thomas was not with the other disciples when they first encountered Jesus after his resurrection from the grave (John 20:24), which understandably made it hard for him to believe. We don't know why he was absent, but God surely knew that his experience of doubt would help us believe.

The fact remains that Thomas had more than the fear of missing out; he did miss out! So, when the other disciples said, "We have seen the Lord" (John 20:25), frankly, he didn't believe them. This is very relatable. The man's associates were making the incredible, world-changing claim that a dead man had come back to life, never to die again. Evidently, they told him that this was a physical resurrection—that the risen Christ had appeared to them in an indestructible body. But Thomas wasn't there, so how could he believe?

Unwilling simply to take his fellow disciples at their word, Thomas wanted Jesus to prove himself, as we sometimes do, especially in the face of death. Thomas said, "Unless I see in his hands the mark of the nails, and place my finger into the mark of the nails, and place my hand into his side, I will never believe" (John 20:25). Thomas wanted to see for himself. He also wanted to touch the Savior's glorified wounds. He wanted what the philosopher Thomas Paine once enviously described as an "ocular and manual demonstration."[2] Otherwise, the disciple declared, he would *never* believe.

Because of his famous nickname, Thomas has the reputation for being the only skeptic of the resurrection. His fatalistic comment after Lazarus died reinforces the popular view that he was an inveterate doubter: "Let us also go, that we may die with him" (John 11:16). We may get the mistaken impression from all this that none of the other disciples doubted, and maybe we think that good Christians never doubt. But, in fact, most of the disciples had trouble believing in the resurrection of the body—or at least the men did. Luke tells us in his Gospel that three days after Jesus was crucified, the eleven original disciples gathered in Jerusalem with other followers of Jesus. They were discussing the testimony of some that Jesus "had risen indeed" (24:34). Suddenly, Jesus was there, standing among them, giving them God's peace. But according to Luke, "they were startled and frightened and thought they saw a spirit" (24:37). The disciples were scared out of their minds, as we would be if someone we knew to be dead suddenly showed up standing next to us.

What Jesus said to these frightened men exposes their spiritual skepticism. He said, "Why are you troubled, and why do doubts

---

2   Thomas Paine, quoted in Jennifer Michael Hecht, *Doubt: A History: The Great Doubters and Their Legacy of Innovation from Socrates and Jesus to Thomas Jefferson and Emily Dickinson* (New York: HarperOne, 2004), 357.

arise in your hearts?" (24:38). It wasn't just Thomas: they all had their doubts.

Similarly, Matthew tells us that later on, when the disciples met Jesus in Galilee, "they worshiped him, but some doubted" (28:17). Matthew's use of the plural indicates that Thomas was not alone in his skepticism. The Greek word he chooses to describe their spiritual struggle is a form of *distazō*, a word that indicates hesitation, such as we sometimes experience when we feel caught between faith and disbelief.

Amazingly, the first disciples had this inner conflict at the very moment when Jesus commanded them to go into all the world and preach the gospel. The Great Commission was given to doubter-believers who worshiped Jesus but also struggled to have faith, even when they were in the physical presence of the risen Christ. Christian Wiman finds this encouraging in his personal struggle to believe the biblical gospel. He writes:

> The Gospels vary quite a bit in their accounts of Jesus' resurrection and the ensuing encounters he had with people, but they are quite consistent about one thing: many of his followers doubted him, sometimes even when he was staring them in the face. This ought to be heartening for those of us who seek belief. If the disciples of Christ could doubt not only firsthand accounts of his resurrection but the very fact of his face in front of them, then clearly, doubt has little to do with distance from events.[3]

---

3 Christian Wiman, *My Bright Abyss: Meditation of a Modern Believer* (New York: Farrar, Straus and Giroux, 2013), 76.

Some interpreters are critical of Thomas's demand for more evidence, but I think we should commend him for his quest to know the truth. When he had his doubts, Thomas did not stop struggling to believe. And at least he was willing to consider the evidence. The notorious atheist Richard Dawkins—who taught evolutionary biology at Oxford and advocated outspokenly for the elimination of the School of Theology—once defined faith as "the great cop-out, the great excuse to evade the need to think and evaluate evidence." He continued, "Faith is belief in spite of, even perhaps because of, the lack of evidence."[4]

Thomas is a good counterexample to Dawkins's dismissive claims. Thomas believed not in spite of the evidence; rather, he insisted on evaluating the evidence fairly for himself so that his belief would be well justified. To that end, he was willing to encounter Jesus, which some skeptics aren't. Thomas was open to the evidence, and open to Jesus.

His example is especially important for anyone who is doubtful about the life, death, and resurrection of Jesus the Christ. Are we willing to weigh the evidence? Truthfully, it is the only intellectually responsible thing to do. There is too much at stake simply to walk away. What is at stake, specifically, is the infinitely valuable possibility of eternal life.

Throughout this book, I have tried to be honest about the doubts that most Christians have, and to grant the freedom to be honest about our doubts. It is not necessarily sinful to be skeptical. But it is wrong to shut the door on God, to have what Barnabas Piper calls "unbelieving doubt"—the perilous perspective of

4   Richard Dawkins, "A Scientist's Case against God" (lecture at the Edinburgh International Science Festival, April 15, 1992), *The Independent*, April 20, 1992, 17.

someone who is unwilling to believe.[5] In his analysis of the story of Thomas, Keith Johnson explains the difference between doubts that honor God and doubts that don't:

> Doubt crosses into sin when a person stops trying to address it. Thomas doubted the resurrection, but he did not sin as he did so. His doubt arose because of his limited knowledge and his inability to make sense of what he heard. He had sincere questions that prevented him from affirming that Christ was alive, and he wanted more information to answer these questions. This is the key: Thomas sought to address the causes of his doubt. He was willing to learn, and he embraced the truth immediately after Jesus appeared to him.[6]

Believing Thomas

Yes, despite his doubts, Thomas did come to faith. When artists portray his famous encounter with Jesus, they often depict the disciple reaching out and touching his wounds. Caravaggio's painting *The Incredulity of Saint Thomas* might be the most famous. Caravaggio's Thomas takes his index finger and probes the fleshy folds of his Savior's side, trying to comprehend what happened to the body of Jesus.

I am not sure Caravaggio's rendering is totally accurate. Certainly, Thomas *said* that he wouldn't believe unless he could put

---

5 Barnabas Piper, *Help My Unbelief: Why Doubt Is Not the Enemy of Faith* (Charlotte: Good Book, 2020), 83.

6 Keith Johnson, "Doubt," in *Life Questions Every Student Asks: Faithful Responses to Common Issues*, ed. Gary M. Burge and David Lauber (Downers Grove, IL: InterVarsity Press, 2020), 137.

his fingers in the nail marks or place his hand in the Savior's sword-wounded side. Maybe he said this because the other disciples told him that this is what they had done when they saw Jesus after he rose from the grave: they handled the evidence for themselves, touching his glorified body. It is also true that Jesus invited Thomas to touch him. "Put your finger here," he said, "and see my hands; and put out your hand, and place it in my side" (John 20:27). His instructions are so specific that Thomas may well have obeyed them.

However, the Bible never says whether Thomas took Jesus up on his invitation and touched his wounds. All that John records is the answer he gave as soon as he was convinced: "My Lord and my God!" For Thomas, seeing was believing, maybe without any touching. This is one of the emotional high points of the Gospels. At the very moment when he became an eyewitness of the risen Lord Jesus Christ, everything within Thomas bowed down and worshiped.

What made this reverent response possible was our Savior's sympathy for skeptics. Jesus did not blame Thomas for his lack of faith or condemn him for his disbelief. He did not hold himself back until the disciple showed him more trust. Instead, Jesus moved toward Thomas in love and said, "Peace be with you" (John 20:26). He held out his hands and invited his friend to step forward in faith. "Do not disbelieve," he said, "but believe" (John 20:27).

Jesus is always moving toward us, especially if we have our doubts. In the face of everything fearful, he says, "Peace be with you." He holds out his hands to welcome us—hands that were pierced with sharp nails for the payment of our sins. He tells us to stop doubting and start believing instead.

The best way to respond is the way Thomas did, not only by seeing and believing but also by worshiping and surrendering. Declare that Jesus of Nazareth is both Lord and God, and then start serving him, as Thomas did. By all accounts, Thomas is the apostle who carried the gospel all the way to India, founding the church that honors his memory there to this day. Keith Johnson rightly concludes: "John's goal is not to portray Thomas as a sinful doubter whose example is to be avoided at all costs. Rather, John presents Thomas as a role model for Christians."[7]

Reasons to Believe

As we scan this story, witnessing Thomas's dramatic encounter with Jesus, there is another group of people we should notice, who appear on the edges of the scene. This is one place in John's Gospel (see also 17:20) that refers to other believers—including us. Jesus said to Thomas: "Have you believed because you have seen me? Blessed are those who have not seen and yet have believed" (20:29). By saying this, Jesus brings us into the picture. He lets us know that he had us in mind when he was dying and rising again. Although we have not yet seen the risen Christ with our own eyes, he invites us to believe in him and then blesses us when we do.

When we read the stories of Thomas and the other disciples, sometimes we envy their firsthand encounters with Jesus. They walked with Jesus and talked with Jesus; if they wanted to, they could touch him. Sometimes, we imagine that it must have been easier for them to believe. Then again, maybe it wasn't, because

7   Johnson, "Doubt," 136.

they had as many doubts as we do. What is certain is that no matter how many doubts we have, if we believe in Jesus, we will be blessed. This is one of God's precious promises to us in the gospel: blessed are those who do not see and yet believe!

The more I read the Gospels, the more I believe in the resurrection of the body.[8] I believe it because the empty tomb is evidence that demands a verdict—a problem that even Pontius Pilate struggled to solve. I believe it because the first eyewitnesses of the resurrection were women—a fact no one in the first century was likely to invent. I believe it because nearly all the apostles sealed their testimony in blood, which they hardly would have done for a hoax.

I find their testimony decidedly credible. Historical claims can only be assessed on the basis of the available evidence. History is yesterday's eyewitness news. Like most things we know from the past, we learn about the crucifixion and the resurrection of Jesus of Nazareth by word of mouth. I like the testimony of the sober-minded fishermen, shrewd tax collectors, and observant doctors who tell us their stories in the biblical Gospels. These men were not gullible but skeptical, which I find reassuring. Their doubts can strengthen our faith. They were as critical as we would have been—maybe more so. They carefully considered the available evidence before stating their convictions. In the end, the living body of Jesus Christ convinced them beyond all possible doubt that he is risen from the dead.

---

8   For a thorough consideration of the evidence for the resurrection of Jesus Christ, see Thomas A. Miller, *Did Jesus Really Rise from the Dead? A Surgeon-Scientist Examines the Evidence* (Wheaton, IL: Crossway, 2013); Frank Morison, *Who Moved the Stone? A Skeptic Looks at the Death and Resurrection of Christ* (1958; repr., Grand Rapids, MI: Zondervan, 1987); and N. T. Wright, *The Resurrection of the Son of God*, Christian Origins and the Question of God 3 (Minneapolis: Fortress, 2003).

All things considered, I agree with Antony Flew, the English philosopher, stubborn evidentialist, and outspoken atheist who, near the end of his life, came unexpectedly to believe that "the evidence for the resurrection is better than for claimed miracles in any other religion. It's outstandingly different in quality and quantity."[9] I also agree with the summary of the old Princeton theologian Charles Hodge, who wrote:

> As the resurrection of Christ is an historical fact, it is to be proved by historical evidence. The apostle therefore appeals to the testimony of competent witnesses. . . . To render such testimony irresistible it is necessary: 1. That the fact to be proved should be of a nature to admit of being certainly known. 2. That adequate opportunity be afforded to the witnesses to ascertain its nature, and to be satisfied of its verity. 3. That the witnesses be of sound mind and discretion. 4. That they be men of integrity. If these conditions be fulfilled, human testimony establishes the truth of a fact beyond reasonable doubt. If, however, in addition to these grounds of confidence, the witnesses give their testimony at the expense of great personal sacrifice, or confirm it with their blood . . . then it is insanity and wickedness to doubt it. All these considerations concur in proof of the resurrection of Christ, and render it the best authenticated event in the history of the world.[10]

9 Antony Flew and Gary R. Habermas, *Did the Resurrection Happen? A Conversation with Gary Habermas and Antony Flew*, ed. David J. Baggett (Downers Grove, IL: InterVarsity Press, 2009), 85.

10 Charles Hodge, *A Commentary on the First Epistle to the Corinthians* (London: Banner of Truth, 1964), 314.

Blessings for Believers

If the testimony of Thomas and the other disciples—both men and women—is true, it makes all the difference in the world. The resurrection of the body means that not even death is outside God's control or has the dreadful power to prevent his eternal purposes for us from coming to pass. From Easter Sunday until the end of the world, we can rest in the hope that our lives are not in vain but will count for eternity.

Now we need to decide how we will respond to this good news. Believing Thomas responded in faith. When he acknowledged the resurrection of Jesus from the dead, he did more than give his intellectual assent to a historical fact. He received Jesus as Savior and surrendered to him as Lord. By the time in the story he says, "My Lord and my God," we readers should be ready to say it too.

Really, this is the point we have been reaching toward throughout this book on faith and doubt—the point not simply of believing but of surrendering to the supreme lordship of Jesus Christ. When we bow down and worship him as the living Son of God and risen Savior of the world, we are blessed.

Thomas could have and probably should have believed simply on the testimony of the other disciples. We should too. For some of us, the problem all along has been that we are not willing to surrender. Barnabas Piper exposes this issue bluntly: "Often the intellectual obstacle to unbelief is a convenient excuse for rebellion."[11] Deep down, we know that Jesus is the Christ. Only we tell ourselves that he isn't—or say that we aren't totally sure—because we don't want to submit to his authority. It isn't an intellectual

11 Piper, *Help My Unbelief*, 33.

problem at all; it's a moral problem. It isn't just what we believe that is at stake; it's what we are willing to do or stop doing. Honestly, we're unwilling to humble our pride, abandon our prejudice, give up our greed, or surrender our sexuality. But when we finally submit to Jesus in faith and obedience, we are greatly blessed.

How are we blessed? We are blessed because we know the Savior, who alone has the power to forgive all our sins. We are blessed because to know him is to know the Father, who loves us and cares for us. We are blessed because the risen Lord Jesus has sent us the Holy Spirit to break the bondage of everything that holds us back from being morally pure and spiritually free. We are blessed because we have a reason to live and a message to proclaim. We are blessed because we know our risen Lord will bring justice into this broken world and heal everything that is sick and wounded. We are blessed because we have an unshakeable hope in our own coming resurrection from the dead. We too will rise again. Because we believe, one day we will see.

The following questions are important for anyone to answer: What faith do I have in the resurrection of the body? Do I trust God for my own resurrection from the grave? And will I believe this for the people I love and one day will lose—the family and friends who die in Christ?

The Presbyterian minister Benjamin Morgan Palmer answered this question at the burial site of his teenage daughter. Palmer and his wife went out to dig her grave, as was the custom. The sad couple were overwhelmed with grief that day. Nineteen years earlier they had lost a newborn son. They went to bury the body of their beloved daughter near the same spot, on the bank of a gentle stream. As they dug into the dirt, they made the unexpected discovery of a lock of their little boy's hair. Here is how Palmer describes the moment:

> The pick-axe and the shovel threw aside the earth, which for many years had pressed upon the bosom of the infant. Only a few bones and a little skull. No, wait a second; and with trembling hand the father clipped one little curl from which the luster had faded, but twining still around the hollow temple. He placed it on the palm of his hand, without a word, before the eye of the mother. With a smothered cry she fell upon his neck. "It is our boy's. I see it as long ago, the soft lock that curled upon his temple." "Take it, Mother; it is to us the prophecy of the resurrection; the grave has not the power to destroy."[12]

Benjamin Palmer did not doubt but believed. He is one of the countless people that Jesus blessed the first time he saw Thomas after his resurrection from the grave. Blessed is *everyone* who believes that Jesus rose again, who knows that *all* God's sons and daughters will rise again, and who says to Jesus, "My Lord and my God!"

---

12 Benjamin M. Palmer, *The Broken Home, or, Lessons in Sorrow*, quoted in James W. Bruce III, *From Grief to Glory: Spiritual Journeys of Mourning Parents* (Wheaton, IL: Crossway, 2002), 124.

So Peter got out of the boat and walked on the water and came to Jesus. But when he saw the wind, he was afraid, and beginning to sink he cried out, "Lord, save me." Jesus immediately reached out his hand and took hold of him, saying to him, "O you of little faith, why did you doubt?"

MATTHEW 14:29–31

10

Doubting Your Doubts

Peter on the Sea of Galilee

AS WE CONSIDER THE LIFE AHEAD OF US, with all its challenges
and possibilities, sometimes we wonder about our next move.
What's the next step—not only educationally, professionally, or
romantically, but also spiritually?

When Christian Wiman considered this question, he had trouble coming up with a clear answer. The poet was drawing near
to faith in Christ. As he came to the precipice of everything he
knew and still wanted to understand, he famously penned these
words of longing, titled "My Bright Abyss":

Once more I come to the edge of all I know
and believing in nothing believe in this:[1]

---

1   In Christian Wiman, *My Bright Abyss: Meditation of a Modern Believer* (New York:
Farrar, Straus and Giroux, 2013), 3.

And that is where Wiman's poem ends—unfinished, with a colon rather than a period after its fourth line—because he was not sure yet what he believed or where his faith would take him. He was on the edge, not knowing where his next step would lead.

We all face similar moments, at the precipice of everything we know. The next step is a big one, maybe more like a leap. It looks like such a long way down that it is hard for us to move. Yet we can't stand still. We all have decisions we need to make, including spiritual decisions. So we have to ask ourselves: What is my next move? What step will I take in my journey with faith and doubt?

One Small Step

Maybe the boldest step that anyone has ever taken—including Neil Armstrong!—is the step Simon Peter took one night on the Sea of Galilee.

The disciples had just witnessed a stupendous miracle: the feeding of five thousand (Matt. 14:13–21). Jesus had wanted some time to himself, grieving as he was over the brutal beheading of his cousin John the Baptist. Together Jesus and his disciples set sail for some quiet shoreline. But Jesus simply could not ignore the huge crowds that wanted to experience his teaching and healing ministry. With tender compassion, he turned back to touch the people who needed his help.

As the day went on, people got hungry, and the disciples grew increasingly impatient to get away. If the Greek language had a word for "hangry," doubtless Matthew would have used it. The disciples really just wanted people to leave them alone. But Jesus continued to care. With the blessing of heaven, he turned five loaves and two fish into enough food to satisfy five thousand men, plus women and children. Truly, it was a miracle—one of the greatest ever performed.

After gathering all the leftovers—yes, leftovers!—the disciples finally had a chance to get away. Jesus dismissed the crowds and then lingered on the shore until he could help the last needy soul who stayed afterward to talk. Then, finally, "he went up on the mountain by himself to pray" (Matt. 14:23). No doubt Jesus was mourning his beloved cousin, and perhaps contemplating the trials and tribulations that lay ahead of him.

Then a storm came up, as storms do on the Sea of Galilee. Matthew tells us—and he would know, because he was there—that "the boat by this time was a long way from the land, beaten by the waves, for the wind was against them" (14:24). In the middle of that black night—around 3:00 a.m.—the disciples saw a strange apparition. It was Jesus coming toward them, striding on the sea. But when they saw him walking on the water, "they were terrified, and said, 'It is a ghost!' and they cried out in fear" (14:26). This was not the first time Jesus needed to reassure his frightened followers, and it wouldn't be the last. Immediately, he said to them, "Take heart; it is I. Do not be afraid" (14:27).

It was at this moment that Peter was inspired to step out in faith. Martin Luther King Jr. rightly said: "Take the first step in faith. You don't have to see the whole staircase."[2] Peter took that first step. He had heard Jesus claim to be the Son of God. He had seen him perform healing miracles. Hours before, he had gathered up the broken pieces of bread that proved Jesus's power to feed the people. Peter surely believed that Jesus could walk on

2 Martin Luther King Jr., quoted by Marian Wright Edelman, "Kids First," *Mother Jones* 16, no. 3 (1991): 77.

water. He also believed that by the power of Jesus, he could walk on water too. So, he blurted out—which was very "on brand" for Peter—"Lord, if it is you, command me to come to you on the water" (14:28). When Jesus invited his disciple to join him on the open sea, Peter "got out of the boat and walked on the water and came to Jesus" (14:29).

This was one of the greatest steps of faith that anyone has ever taken. It was the first time Peter had ever seen anyone walk on water. In fact, it was the first time that *anyone* had ever seen anyone walk on water. Yet, as soon as Peter saw this, he had the faith to believe that he too could deny the physics of aquatics. He swung one leg out of the boat, then the other. Not doubting or hesitating, he trusted Jesus to hold him up and make him stand. This was one small step for a disciple, and one giant leap for discipleship. Someone who is willing to step out onto stormy waters is willing to take *any* step that Jesus asks him or her to take.

Stepping Out

For the rest of his life, Peter had something amazing to put on his résumé, or to use when people asked him for "two truths and a lie." He was one of only two human beings ever to stride on the sea. This gave his friends something to say as well if anyone complained they were making it sound like Peter could walk on water. "Well, come to think of it, he *did* walk on water. Have I ever told you that story?"

What happened specifically to Peter was unprecedented and unrepeatable. But this narrative can shape our own spiritual story. Peter saw an opportunity—a place where he was invited to walk with Jesus. For him, this place was the Sea of Galilee, one dark and stormy night. For us, it will be some other place. It will be a relationship we know we should pursue, or an educational opportunity that will sharpen our gifts, or a conversation we need to have, or a call to ministry, or some other door that suddenly opens right in front of us. It may be something we always hoped would happen. Or it may be as unexpected as seeing Jesus walking on the water next to our boat. But whatever it is, we feel a sudden prompting to do something next in our walk with God.

With that inner prompting comes a divine invitation. It may not come through an audible voice, although it certainly could. However it is given, we receive the same simple invitation that Peter received when Jesus said, "Come." There are times when Jesus says, "Go," as he did when he gave his disciples their Great Commission at the end of Matthew's Gospel. But wherever Jesus wants us to go, he also plans to be right there with us. So the command he usually gives to his disciples is "Come, follow me."

The question for each of us is what we will do when Jesus gives us this invitation. When the Son of God says, "Come," will we climb out of the relative safety of our boat and follow him the way Peter did? Will we at least take the next step he is asking us to take? Joni Eareckson Tada famously says: "Faith isn't the ability to believe long and far into the misty future. It's simply taking God at his word and taking the next step."[3]

When Jesus calls us to "come," we never know exactly what we are getting ourselves into. We will have to trust therefore that God knows what he is doing, that he has our best interests at heart. Lesslie Newbigin wisely says, "Christian faith is not a matter of

---

3 Joni Eareckson Tada, quoted in Barnabas Piper, *Help My Unbelief: Why Doubt Is Not the Enemy of Faith* (Charlotte: Good Book, 2020), 44.

logically demonstrable certainties but of the total commitment of fallible human beings putting their trust in the faithful God who has called them."[4]

To be honest, we all have our doubts in life—even those of us who believe. We have seen this throughout our study on faith and doubt. Most of the believers we meet in the Bible—like most Christians we meet in real life—sometimes find it hard to believe. We have trouble taking God at his word. We are unsure about his calling for our lives, and uncertain about his willingness to heal us or care for us. We doubt whether he will protect us or provide for us.

But when we do take a step of faith, we find—as Peter did—that climbing out of the boat is neither as risky as it seems nor as foolhardy as some people have said, but one of the best decisions we could ever make. The friendship we form turns out to be life-changing. The education we receive is ideal preparation for future service to the kingdom of God. The Holy Spirit empowers us to do more in the marketplace or in ministry than we ever imagined. The next step is the right step because Jesus is right there beside us. To capture the full scope of what happens when we decide to follow Jesus, the evangelist Luis Palau often said, "One encounter with Jesus Christ is enough to change you, instantly, forever."[5]

When we walk with Jesus, we discover that he is everything he promised to be, and everything we need. He keeps his word. He empowers us to fulfill our calling. He protects us from many dangers. He generously provides what we need. He keeps us in his

---

4 Lesslie Newbigin, *Proper Confidence: Faith, Doubt, and Certainty in Christian Disciple-ship* (Grand Rapids, MI: Eerdmans, 1995), 99.

5 As shared by Kevin Palau, email message to author, November 6, 2023.

loving care and heals the deep wounds in our hearts. Jesus proves his righteous mercy to us as we walk with him.

Why Peter Faltered

And then we start to sink. At least, this is what happened to Peter. He stepped out in faith. He walked on water, literally. He made it all the way to Jesus. But then he made the mistake of looking at the storm instead of looking at Jesus. His faith gave way, and he started sinking.

Most of us can relate—maybe all of us. The Bible tells us to "ask in faith, with no doubting, for the one who doubts is like a wave of the sea that is driven and tossed by the wind" (James 1:6). Yet most of us do get driven by our doubts. We are believers, yes, but many times we are doubter-believers who struggle to be consistent. We do believe, but God help us with our unbelief!

Christian Wiman writes about this as well. As the poet considers his faith journey, there are days when he says to himself, "*It is not working for me.*" What Wiman means by this is that sometimes he has the same struggles that he used to have before he started believing again that Jesus died on the cross and rose from the grave. "The turn towards God has not lessened my anxieties," he writes, "and I find myself continually falling back into wounds, wishes, terrors I thought I had risen beyond."[6]

What terrified Peter was the surrounding storms. When he saw the wind around him whipping the waves beneath him, he started to panic and stopped trusting Jesus to hold him up. Sooner or later, something similar will happen to us. The winds and the

---

6   Wiman, *My Bright Abyss*, 9.

waves that threatened to drown Peter in the Sea of Galilee are a metaphor for the turbulent waters that we all face. Life is full of sudden setbacks. Before we can walk through an open door, it slams shut. A broken relationship feels like the end of a dream. Money worries cause constant anxiety. Then our faith falters, and we start to sink.

Peter's story warns us about the faith struggles we may continue to face even after we make our next spiritual move. Earlier I said that Peter took one of the boldest steps that anyone has ever taken. But I also need to acknowledge that his exercise in spiritual courage lasted less than a minute! How soon will we face our next crisis of faith? And what will we do when it happens?

The Benefits of the Doubt

Maybe the most important part of this story is what happened next. We might think that Peter's big, bold step out of the boat was the most important thing described in Matthew 14. Certainly, it is important to answer the call of Christ, no matter how impossible it seems to do what God is asking us to do.

But most believers do not take one bold step after another. In fact, I'm not sure any of us do. The courageous Christians we meet in the Scriptures usually take missteps. They stumble and fall. They backtrack or take the long way around before they reach their final destination. So, the main question for most of us is not whether we will step out of the boat but what we will do when we start to sink.

Notice what Peter did. He reached for Jesus. He asked for help. He cried out, "Lord, save me" (v. 30). What we do when Jesus calls us to come is important, but so is what we say when we start to sink. What Peter said was simply this: "Help me, Jesus!"

Sooner or later, every one of us will need as much help as Peter did. We will find ourselves in trouble and won't know which way to turn. We will have a problem too big for us or anyone else to solve—a test we cannot pass, a task we cannot perform, a heart we cannot heal. When this inevitably happens, our first impulse should be to do what Peter did and cry out to the Son of God, who is also the Savior of the world. Jesus saves!

When Peter cried out, Jesus responded immediately. He did two things for his disciple that we might describe as Peter getting "the benefit of the doubt." It would have been much better for Peter never to doubt at all, of course, but simply to keep trusting Jesus and walking with him on the water. Yet, when he started to sink, Jesus stepped in to help him, and so his disciple benefited from his experience with doubt. Peter is not alone in this regard. Many people benefit from their doubts. The Scottish pastor and novelist George MacDonald testified:

> A man may be haunted with doubts, and only grow thereby in faith. Doubts are the messengers of the Living One to rouse the honest. They are the first knock at our door of things that are not yet, but have to be, understood. . . . Doubt must precede every deeper assurance; for uncertainties are what we first see when we look into a region hitherto unknown, unexplored.[7]

7 George MacDonald, *Unspoken Sermons: Series I, II, III in One Volume* (n.p.: NuVision, 2007), 191.

So how did Peter benefit from his doubts? First, Jesus stabilized his disciple to keep him from drowning. Matthew says, "Jesus immediately reached out his hand and took hold of him" (14:31). Peter's doubts didn't sink him, because Jesus was there to save him. Whenever we are in real danger—whether physical or spiritual—we can trust Jesus to protect us. In our moments of greatest need, if we reach out for Jesus, he will reach out for us and hold on to us. He will grasp us and never let us go, even when we start to let go of him. One of the benefits of Peter's doubt was finding greater security in the strong grip of his Savior. "Never will I leave you," Jesus says; "never will I forsake you" (Heb. 13:5 NIV).

Then Jesus gave Peter a second benefit—the blessing of holding him to a higher standard. Jesus said, "O you of little faith, why did you doubt?" (Matt. 14:31; cf. 8:26). At first, this may seem rather harsh. Of all the disciples, Peter had the *most* faith, not the least. He was the only one who stepped out on the stormy waters. Yet Jesus knew that Peter would face much greater challenges in the coming years: temptation, oppression, imprisonment, and finally martyrdom. Rather than simply commending him for taking one little step of faith, Jesus challenged Peter to start exercising a bigger, bolder faith—the kind that one day would move mountains (see Matt. 21:21).

To that end, Jesus gave his disciple a question to ponder—which was such a gift! "Why did you doubt?" Jesus asked. I imagine Peter pondering this question later that day and then reflecting on it from time to time in the following years. Why *did* he doubt the call of Jesus, the presence of Jesus, and the power of Jesus to hold him up on the stormy seas?

By asking this good question, Jesus was inviting Peter to doubt his doubts. Was there any good reason for him to doubt the saving grace or the supernatural power of the Son of God? No, there wasn't. Both his personal experience with Jesus and the plain teaching of the word of God gave Peter every reason to believe. So rather than doubting his step of faith, he needed to subject his doubts to the careful scrutiny of biblically informed skepticism.

Doubting our doubts: this is a healthy habit of mind for anyone who sometimes struggles to believe in Jesus. It is also a good way for us to help the skeptics we love. Philip Yancey writes about a close friend who was agnostic about the claims of Christ and doubtful about the pretensions of the Christians he knew. He was especially scornful of the popular question "What would Jesus do?" In protest, he started asking, "What would an atheist do?" Soon he had to stop, however, because he discovered that he didn't like the answers he was getting.[8] His skepticism had taken a dangerous turn, at least for an atheist: it was leading him toward God rather than away from him. This is what happens when we start to doubt our doubts.

Of course, we all have our doubts, including the same wide range of doubts we encounter in stories from the Bible. But we also have many good reasons to believe that Jesus of Nazareth led a life of faithful obedience to God, that he died as an innocent man on a bloody cross, and that he came back from the grave in a body of immortal splendor. We have good reasons to believe that Jesus has promised to be with us to the end of the age and that he will return to rescue us in glorious triumph. Therefore,

8   Philip Yancey, *A Skeptic's Guide to Faith: What It Takes to Make the Leap* (Grand Rapids, MI: Zondervan, 2009), 19.

we should be extremely skeptical of any suggestion that Jesus is not the Son of God and the Savior of the world, that he is not a very present help in trouble, that his Spirit is unable to break the bondage of remaining sin, or that he lacks the power to save us. In other words, we should be skeptical of anything that Satan wants us to believe instead of the gospel.

Part of doubting our doubts is remembering what we know to be true. Tom Skinner—a preacher at the forefront of black evangelicalism in the 1970s—once said:

> I spent a long time trying to come to grips with my doubts, when suddenly I realized I had better come to grips with what I believe. I have since moved from the agony of questions that I cannot answer, to the reality of answers that I cannot escape . . . and it's a great relief.[9]

Peter found that relief. So did the men and women we have met in the pages of this book, and we can find it too. After further reflection, and upon closer investigation, Peter would conclude that he was right when he trusted God for his next step and wrong when he sank down under the weight of sudden doubts. When we doubt our doubts instead of doubting God, we will reach the same conclusion. Rather than holding back or falling down, we will step out in faith and keep walking with Jesus.

In her remarkable narrative "Escape from Kabul," Sarah Eekhoff Zylstra recounts the terrible plight of Christians who were trapped after the 2020 withdrawal of US troops from Afghanistan. Pastor

---

9 Tom Skinner, quoted by Dennis Rainey, "My Struggle with Unbelief," Family Life, 2006, https://www.familylife.com/, accessed November 22, 2023.

Ramazan was desperate to escape from the Taliban with his wife and young children. Because they were registered Christians, they feared for their very lives. For weeks they were on the run, in hiding, until finally they were able to catch a flight out of Kabul. What gave them the hope to persevere was Peter's experience with Jesus. Ramazan says:

> All those moments, every second, he was with us. I was think-ing about Matthew 14, when Jesus asked his disciples to go to [the] other side of the sea, in the middle of the sea. There was a storm, there was darkness, there was fear. And they thought, "We're going to die." But Jesus was walking right in that time, right in that moment, in the middle of the darkness, in the middle of the difficulties. I was, during these two months, I was thinking the same thing: "Where's God?" But immediately I was thinking about that part of the Gospel of Matthew, "God is here; focus on Jesus, not on difficulties."[10]

Focusing on Jesus: this was the life lesson that Peter learned one night on the Sea of Galilee. It is the most important lesson we all need to learn in our ongoing struggle with unbelief. When we focus on Jesus, faith overcomes all our doubts, and we find ourselves able to walk with Jesus, step by step.

---

10 Ramazan, quoted in Sarah Eeckhoff Zylstra, "Escape from Kabul," TGC, April 29, 2022, https://www.thegospelcoalition.org/.

General Index

ability, 7, 37
abortion, 84
Abraham, 18–19, 25
abundance, 70, 71, 74, 79
abuse, 87, 102, 123
Adam, 2, 6, 15, 24
Adams, Douglas, 100
addiction, 87, 123
Afghanistan, 164
agnosticism, 14, 87, 163
angels, 54–55, 56, 59
anxiety, 126, 159, 160
apologetics, 33
Armstrong, Neil, 154
arrogance, 84
Asaph, 81–97
assurance, 11, 18, 24, 37, 161
atheism, 14, 64, 87, 142, 147, 163
authenticity, 9, 54, 86

Barna Group, 130
Bavinck, Herman, 2–3, 30, 91–92
belief, 12, 40, 125, 129, 141–42. *See also* faith
believers, 159
Bible
    confidence in, 5

as reliable, 3
study of, 7–8
teachings of, 10
truth of, 9
biblical ethics, 5
biblical scholarship, 8
bitterness, 68, 85
blessings, 74–75, 148–50
Boaz, 71, 74
Bonhoeffer, Dietrich, 42, 109
Book of Common Prayer, 107–8
Brunson, Andrew, 114–15
Buechner, Frederick, 104, 127
burning bush, 35–38, 44

calling, 158
Calvin, John, 10–11, 21–22, 106, 111
cancer, 89
Caravaggio, 143
celebrity culture, 84
cherubim, 59
China, 52
Christian life, 33, 127
chronic illness, 68, 122
church, 73–74, 90, 91
Civil War Museum, 17–18

classical apologetics, 33
compassion, 123, 154
complaining, 68, 111
Compline, 107–8
confession of faith, 124–25
consolation, 77
crucifixion, 115, 146
cursing, 111–112

danger, 162
dark night of the soul, 99–100, 104, 113
David, 8, 54, 59–60, 76, 82, 105
Dawkins, Richard, 142
death, 93, 110, 132, 137
deliverance, 133
demons, 120, 132
Depeche Mode, 99
depression, 48
despair, 77, 111, 129
desperation, 121, 123
disability, 40
disappointment, 71
disaster, 63–64
disbelief, 141
disciples, 120, 121, 139, 140, 145
discipleship, 42, 156
discouragement, xiii, 48, 88–89, 101
dishonesty, 6
disobedience, 6, 127
distazō, 141
Dostoevsky, Fyodor, 101
doubter-believers, 159
"Doubting Thomas," 34, 139–45
doubts
    benefits of, 160–65
    calling out of, 22–24
    and discouragement, 88–89
    doubting of, 163–64
    and faith, 126

of God's word, 1–15
    honesty about, 34, 41
    of Sarah, 18–21, 22–24
    as spiritual, xi

Ecuador, 58
Elimelech, 65
Eliot, T. S., 99
Elisha, 49–51, 53–57
Elizabeth, 25
Elliot, Elisabeth, 20, 58
Elliot, Jim, 58
empathy, 74, 121
empty tomb, 30, 75, 116, 132, 146
encouragement, 24, 43
enemies, 49–53, 56, 57–58, 107
epilepsy, 120
Esau, 54
eternal life, 31
evangelicals, 5, 48, 164
Eve, 2, 3–4, 6, 15, 24, 31, 34
evidence, 142, 147
evil, 64–65, 72, 83, 84
exorcism, 120
eyewitness, 144

failure, 34
fairness, 87
faith
    certainty of, 12
    as credible, xii
    crisis of, 82, 110–11
    and disbelief, 141
    and doubt, xi, 126
    of Eve, 15
    and evidence, 142
    as genuine, 134
    as gift, 128
    importance of, 82
    life of, 33
    steps of, 156, 158

false prophet, 103
fear, 39, 48, 52, 53, 165
fearless, 56–60
fear of missing out (FOMO), 85
feeding of the five thousand,
    154–55
Fitzgerald, F. Scott, 99
Fleming, Olive, 58
Fleming, Pete, 58
Flew, Antony, 147
forgiveness, 31, 94
fullness, 71
future hope, 31

garden of Eden, 3, 24, 25, 103, 121
garden of Gethsemane, 9, 51
Generation Z, 47
George, Timothy, 11
glossophobia, 39
God
    army of, 55
    existence of, 6
    fairness of, 88, 95
    generosity of, 64, 65, 67, 68, 71,
        74, 75, 77
    goodness of, 20, 64, 70, 78, 79,
        83, 96–97, 108
    moral authority of, 4
    patience of, 70, 129
    presence of, xii, 89, 91, 96, 114
    promises of, 18–22
    protection of, 53–56, 57
    silence of, 114
gospel, 15, 57, 58, 125
Graham, Billy, 13–14, 133
gratitude, 74
Gray, Patrick, 27–28
Great Commission, 141, 157
"Great Is Thy Faithfulness," 115
greed, 149
guilt, 128

"hangry," 154
happiness, 86, 87
healing, 31, 124, 130–34
"He Gets Us" marketing campaign,
    22
Heidelberg Catechism, 56–57
historical evidence, 8, 9, 147
history, 11, 19, 146
Hodge, Charles, 147
Holy Spirit
    ministry of, 105
    power of, 14, 49, 139, 158
    presence of, xi, 91
    and the resurrection, 40
    testimony of, 10–11, 23
homosexuality, 5
"honest questions," 5, 26
honesty, 3, 34, 41, 83, 142
hope, 23, 31, 77–79, 93, 95, 149
hopelessness, 48
hospitality, 58
Huaorani, 58–59
human sexuality, 52

illness, 68, 122
imprisonment, 105–9, 114, 162
incarnation, 26, 30
India, 52, 145
injustice, 52, 88, 94
intellectual assent, 148
Isaac, 28
Isaiah, 36

Jacob, 54
James, 75
Jeremiah, 34, 100–114
Jesus Christ
    betrayal of, 51
    blood of, 91
    death and resurrection of, 72, 94,
        115, 142, 146

divinity of, 22
faithfulness of, 44
as fulfillment of promises, 30
lordship of, 148
obedience of, 163
presence of, 41
resurrection of, 131–32, 139
suffering of, 73
Job, 42, 86, 105
John of the Cross, St., 99
Johnson, Keith, 69–70, 75–76, 122, 123, 126, 143
John the Baptist, 25, 154
Jonah, 105
joy, 68, 79
judgment, 6, 30, 44, 94, 95, 100, 101, 102, 103
justice, 6, 85, 92, 93

Keller, Tim, 72–73, 76–77, 94
Kidner, Derek, 112
King, Martin Luther, Jr., 155
King, Stephen, 99

lament, 101, 102, 111
laughter, 28–30
Lazarus, 140
L'Engle, Madeleine, 26
Lewis, C. S., 9–10, 64
life experiences, 20, 21
Linthicum, Robert, 52
logical syllogism, 64
Lord of the Rings, The, 77, 133
loss, 66, 71, 137
love, 58, 132
Lukich, Taisiia, 137–38
Luther, Martin, 15

MacDonald, George, 43, 73, 161
marriage, 6, 129
martyrdom, 59, 162

Mary (mother of Jesus), 26–27, 28, 31
McCully, Ed, 58
McCully, Marilou, 58
McLaughlin, Eric, 77–79
Meade, George G., 17
mercy, xiii, 58, 69–70
Milton, John, 55
miracles, 11, 35, 39, 122, 138, 147, 154–55
missional call, 34, 40, 43–44
Moabites, 66
Mocan, Liviu, 13
mockery, 29, 102
modern science, 13
money, 86, 160
Morrison, Van, 99
Moses, 27, 34–40, 41–44
Most Holy Place, 91
mystery, 100, 108

Naomi, 65–77
Nazis, 109
neutrality, 4, 7
Newbigin, Lesslie, 7, 12, 42, 157–58
noetic effects, of sin, 7
North Korea, 52

obedience, 10, 30, 42, 44, 127, 163
O'Connor, Flannery, 100
omnipotence, 124
Operation Auca, 58
oppression, 52, 87, 94, 162
Orpah, 66, 67
orphans, 87

pain, 64, 138
Paine, Thomas, 140
Palau, Luis, 158
Palmer, Benjamin Morgan, 149–50
panic, 51, 159

paradox, 126
Pashhur, 100
Paul, 11, 108, 128
persecution, 87
personal safety, 47
Peter, 9, 34, 154–65
Peterson, Andrew, 51–52
Pew Research Center, 128–29
Pharaoh, 34, 35, 37, 38, 44
Pilate, Pontius, 146
pilgrimage, xiii, 27, 33
Piper, Barnabas, 40, 128, 129–30, 142–43, 148
poor, 87, 94
pornography, 129
praise, 78, 106, 110
prayer, 75, 104–5, 109, 111, 119, 127, 129
prejudice, 149
pride, 149
prison, 105–9, 114
promise, 17–18, 21, 25
proof, 12
public humiliation, 112
public speaking, 39

question mark, 112–16
Quirinius, 8

racial justice, 6
Ramazan, 165
rebellion, 40, 58
repentance, 95
restoration, 77
resurrection, 30, 115, 131–32, 146, 149, 150
reward, 94
righteousness, 83, 86, 94
Russia, 137
Ruth, 66, 67, 69, 70, 71, 74, 76

sadness, 48
"Safety-ism," 47
Saint, Marjorie, 58
Saint, Nate, 58
salvation
    from eternity, 114
    history of, 19
    hope in, 95
    promises of, 21
    story of, 44
Sarah, 18–21, 22–24, 28–30, 31, 34
sarcasm, 21, 24
Satan, 3, 4, 51, 103, 121
science, 13
Scripture. See Bible
security, 53, 162
self-doubt, 36–40
selfishness, 85, 86
self-promotion, 84
self-righteousness, 58
September 11 terrorist attacks, 47
seraphim, 59
Sevareid, Eric, xii
sexuality, 52, 84, 149
sexual sin, 6, 86
signs, 39, 71
Silas, 108
sin, 7, 95, 125
Skeesuck, Justin, 27–28
skepticism, 5, 7, 23, 64, 125, 130, 140, 144, 163
Skinner, Tom, 164
social injustice, 52
solitary confinement, 104, 114
spiritual journey, 28
spiritual struggle, 88
Sudan, 52
suffering, 64, 72, 73, 77, 103, 104, 112–16

suicide, 87, 93, 112
surveillance, 50, 52
sympathy, 128
Syria, 49–51

Tada, Joni Eareckson, 157
Talbot, Mark, 103, 110–11
Taliban, 165
Templeton, Charles, 14
temptation, 86, 162
Thomas, 34, 139–45, 150
Tolkien, J. R. R., 133
Tolstoy, Leo, 93
Turkey, 52
Turner, Gracie, 48

Ukraine, 137
unbelief, 12, 29, 76–79, 124–29,
    159, 165
"unbelieving doubt," 142–43
uncertainty, 124, 126
unclean spirit, 120, 130
ungodliness, 84, 85, 86, 92
Updike, John, 1–2

verbal abuse, 102
Voltaire, 63–64

walking on water, 156
warfare, 87
Warren, Tish Harrison, 103–4,
    107–8, 131–32
wealth, 85, 92
Wheaton College, 12–13, 114,
    133
wicked, 83, 85, 92, 96
widows, 87
Wiman, Christian, 28, 89–90, 126,
    130, 141, 153–54, 159
word of God, 1–15, 20, 103
worship, 89, 91, 92, 106, 109

Yancey, Philip, 125, 163
Youderian, Barbara, 58
Youderian, Roger, 58

Zechariah (New Testament figure),
    25
Zylstra, Sarah Eekhoff, 164–65

Scripture Index

Genesis
2:16–17......3
3............6
3:1............xiv, 3
3:2............4
3:3............4
3:4–5........4
3:6............5
3:9............7
3:15..........15, 24
3:20..........15
3:21..........15
4:1............15
12:3..........18
16:2..........20
16:3..........20
17:5..........18
18............19
18:9..........19
18:10........19
18:11........19
18:12........19, 20, 25
18:13........19, 23
18:13–14....16
18:14........23, 27
18:15........23
21............25
21:1..........25

21:1–2......25
21:6–7......29
32:1–2......54

Exodus
3:4............36
3:6............37
3:10..........35
3:11..........32
3:12..........38
3:13..........35
3:14..........38
3:18..........38
4:1............39
4:10..........39
4:11–12......40
4:13..........36
4:16..........41
4:17..........41
5:1............41

Leviticus
20:9..........112
24:13–16....112

Ruth
book of.......76
1:8–9.........66

1:11–13......67
1:16–17......69
1:19..........67
1:20–21......62, 67
1:22..........71
2:19–20......74
4:15..........76
4:16..........71

2 Kings
6..............49
6:9–10......50
6:11..........50
6:12..........50
6:13–14......51
6:15..........46, 51
6:16..........53
6:17..........56
6:18–23......57

Job
1:21..........105
7:11..........86
38:4..........12

Psalms
10:1..........70
10:17........70
13:1..........70
13:6..........71
27:3..........60
27:5..........60
34:7..........54
57.............105
68:17........54
73.............82, 83, 90, 92, 95, 97
73:1..........82, 83
73:2..........81, 83, 90
73:2–3.......80
73:2–14......82, 88
73:3..........83

73:4–9.......84
73:4–12......90
73:10........84
73:11........84
73:12........85
73:13–14....85
73:15........88
73:16–17....89
73:17........92
73:18–20....92
73:21–22....95
73:23–24....95
73:25–28....96
73:27........92
73:28........96
77:7–8.......21
91:11–12....54
108:11.......70

Proverbs
25:21........57

Isaiah
6:8............12, 36
7:14..........26

Jeremiah
1:5............113
1:8............103
11:18–21....102
15:21........103
18:22–23....102
20.............101, 104, 111, 112,
             113
20:7..........101, 102, 105
20:7–8.......102
20:10........101, 102
20:11........106
20:11–13....105
20:12........107
20:13........108, 111

20:14 111
20:14–17 110
20:18 . . . . 98, 112
21 113

Lamentations
3:22–23 113

Jonah
2 105

Matthew
book of 157, 165
4:19 10
5:2ff. 10
8:26 162
14 . . . . 160, 165
14:13–21 154
14:23 155
14:24 155
14:26 155
14:27 155
14:28 156
14:29 156
14:29–31 152
14:30 160
14:31 162
16:15 12
17:19–20 120
18:20 91
21:21 162
26:47 51
27:46 . . . . 105, 115
28:17 141
28:20 41

Mark
book of 120, 129, 131
1:17 42
3:15 120
6:7 120

6:13 120
9 . . . . 119, 122, 123, 125,
           130, 131, 132
9:17–18 120
9:19 123
9:20 120
9:21–22 121
9:22 123
9:23 124
9:23–24 118
9:24 . . . . 125, 126
9:25 131
9:26 131
9:27 131
9:29 132
16:4 131

Luke
book of 25
1:30–33 26
1:35 26
1:37 27
1:38 27
2:2 8
24:34 140
24:37 140
24:38 141

John
6:35 . . . . 38n1
8:12 . . . . 38n1
10:9 . . . . 38n1
10:11 . . . . 38n1
11:16 140
11:25 . . . . 38n1
14:6 . . . . 38n1
15:1 . . . . 38n1
17:20 145
20:24 139
20:25 . . . . 139, 140
20:26 144

20:27.........136, 144
20:29.........145

Acts
16:25.........108

Romans
5:10 58
8:28 72
12:20.........57

2 Corinthians
1:20 30

Ephesians
1:4.............114
2:10 114
3:20 27
6:12 53

Colossians
2:2.............11

2 Timothy
3:15 11
3:16 10

Hebrews
book of.......28
3:12 125
10:19–22 91
11:11.........28
12:2 72
12:22–24 91
13:5 ....38, 162

James
1:5.............75
1:6.............75

1 Peter
5:8.............121

2 Peter
1:21 10

Jude
22.............xiii, 70, 128

Revelation
21:8 125

Also Available from Philip Ryken

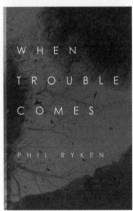

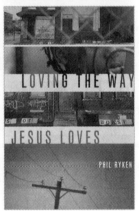

For more information, visit **crossway.org**.